D0035638

HOW TO MAKE A
MILLION DOLLARS
WITH YOUR VOICE
(or Lose Your Tonsils Trying)

GARY OWENS
AND
JEFF LENBURG

New York   Chicago   San Francisco   Lisbon   London   Madrid   Mexico City
Milan   New Delhi   San Juan   Seoul   Singapore   Sydney   Toronto

The McGraw·Hill Companies

Library of Congress Cataloging-in-Publication Data

Owens, Gary.
    How to make a million dollars with your voice (or lose your tonsils trying) /
Gary Owens and Jeff Lenburg.
       p.   cm.
    ISBN 0-07-142410-5 (alk. paper)
    1. Television announcing.   2. Radio announcing.   3. Television advertising.
4. Radio advertising.   5. Voice-overs.   6. Public speaking.   I. Lenburg, Jeff.
II. Title.

    PN1992.8.A6094   2004
    791.4502'8'023—dc22   2003028196

Copyright © 2005 by Gary Owens and Jeff Lenburg. All rights reserved. Printed in the
United States of America. Except as permitted under the United States Copyright Act of
1976, no part of this publication may be reproduced or distributed in any form or by any
means, or stored in a database or retrieval system, without the prior written permission of
the publisher.

2 3 4 5 6 7 8 9 0   FGR/FGR   3 2 1 0 9 8 7 6 5 4

ISBN 0-07-142410-5

McGraw-Hill books are available at special quantity discounts to use as premiums and
sales promotions, or for use in corporate training programs. For more information, please
write to the Director of Special Sales, Professional Publishing, McGraw-Hill, Two Penn
Plaza, New York, NY 10121-2298. Or contact your local bookstore.

This book is printed on acid-free paper.

To the many friends who have made my life so rewarding, especially my family—my wife, Arleta; our sons, Scott and Chris; and my mother and sister—for believing in me. And a special pat to our cats, Squeek and Jasper, for bringing in the paper every morning. Love you all.

Gary Owens

To Holly, for all the joy and laughter.

Jeff Lenburg

Contents

Foreword

LET ME START by saying Gary Owens is without a doubt "a man for all seasons." I know you'll agree when you read his many credits that contribute to his magnificent career in show business, which started at age sixteen in radio and seventeen in television.

Gary and his wife, Arleta, met in college. They have two sons, Scott Michael and Christopher Dane Owens, grown-up lads who, like their father, are in the entertainment business.

I won't attempt to list all of Gary's credits but will instead tally the numbers for you. He's appeared in over one thousand network television shows, more than three thousand animated cartoon episodes, and he's hosted more than twelve thousand national and local radio shows. He's also narrated more than thirty thousand commercials and promos.

Gary is a good friend,* and I've been fortunate to work with him on a number of projects. He's one of the few actors and comedians who can really do "improvisation," which is never rehearsed but is done now! There are people we know who always are fun to be around and always have something good to say about the other guy. That's Gary. The best therapy

---

*In a recent interview in *Radio & Records* magazine, Jonathan Winters said his two best friends in show business are Robin Williams and Gary Owens, a fact that makes Gary very proud.

in the world is laughter, and when and if you should run into Gary Owens, all your troubles will disappear—at least until you get to the parking lot!

Gary, this book is long overdue. I hope you make another million with it and it makes enough for you to pick up the check next time we have lunch.

Always,
Jonathan Winters

Jonathan Winters, as Maude Frickert on the set of a "Bob Hope Special," explains to Gary her recipe for sugar-coated mice.

Preface

THIS BOOK IS a labor of love. I do not use a computer. The entire text was scrawled on butcher paper with a chicken claw, then transferred by hooded scribes using an Underwood manual typewriter, and then blotted. It was tough but it was worth it.

Since the beginning of time, people have made careers with their voice. There were town criers, proclamation readers, railroad conductors who would shout, "Next stop, Scranton!," and professional yodelers. In Switzerland in 1883, a group of these people stood on a mountaintop outside Zurich. They yodeled their message, and when they heard their echo, they were the first people to ask for residuals. That was the very tough Swiss Yodelers Union.

As a youth, I got my first radio gig at sixteen. At that time in my life, I was unsure of what I wanted to do. I was floundering (I had four flounders in my school backpack and two in my pocket). I was considering other careers, perhaps becoming an artist, also tinkering with a job as a fetlock wholesaler or a vocation in a local factory preserving and restoring underwear. I was torn.

Like Dustin Hoffman in that famous "plastic scene" in *The Graduate*, I had a life-altering moment. At my folks' pool party, a relative sidled up to me, pulled me aside, and said the words "Shoelace nibs!" I ignored crazy Uncle Norbert, gave him a Cheez Whiz, and chose a career in radio and television. I never looked back.

I love what I do and I've been very fortunate: people have actually paid me substantial weekly checks to say the words *flurg, foonman, fnork,* and *nurny*. I've worked in many different industries—radio, television, motion pictures, commercials, cartoons, emceeing, public speaking, and more. I have been a national disc jockey for many years—played every genre of music, spun records of nearly every major music notable, from the Beatles to Tony Bennett. I've done television series, specials, sitcoms, and variety shows, performing sketches with Jonathan Winters and John Wayne. I've voiced thousands of animated cartoons, videos, and DVDs, pitched some thirty thousand products in commercials for radio and television, and narrated dozens of audiobooks. I've also recorded fifteen albums and CDs and have served as master of ceremonies for thousands of events as diverse as charity banquets and premieres of major Hollywood movies.

I was inducted into the National Radio Hall of Fame in 1995, the National Association of Broadcasters Hall of Fame (NAB—the biggest broadcast organization in the world) in 1995, and the NAB's TV Hall of Fame in 2002. I'm so fortunate to have a star on the Hollywood Walk of Fame (next to Walt Disney) and have had the opportunity and fun to work with countless celebrities, among them Frank Sinatra, Madonna, Tim Conway, Diana Ross, Ronald Reagan, Jimmy Stewart, and Meatloaf.

This book is my opportunity to give something back. A chance to pass on my knowledge to those who have the skill and desire, and who want a shot at a career in voice and broadcasting. I will share tips of the trade and reveal industry secrets. (Unfortunately, these are secrets of the linoleum and corrugated box industries, but useful nevertheless.) I'll cover the whole process of getting started, from creating a classic voice to breaking into the business, finding an agent, and auditioning for your first job. Also the numerous career opportunities that exist for your voice: disc jockeying, newscasting, sportscasting, weather forecasting, commercials, animated cartoons, television announcing, narration, emceeing, public speaking, and other voice-over opportunities where your voice can be worth a fortune, such as voice messaging and talking toys.

It is a wide range of voicedom. It's a wonderful, wide-open, eclectic mix. Be flexible. In a single day, you may be called to record the voice of the Energizer Bunny, do a radio commercial for a "proven medicated itch fighter," and that night, emcee a rock concert, where you will beseech the crowd to "put your hands together for Limp Bizkit!" We've come a long way from the town crier shouting, "Eight o'clock and all's well."

There's money to be made, there's glory to be had, there's wolf pudding and porcupine fritters to be eaten. (Many radio stations and recording studios have rather odd snack areas.)

For the past four decades, I have known and worked with numerous gifted performers. Many of them have contributed their talents and expertise to the chapters in this book. They include people who are having amazing careers, such as Vin Scully, Willard Scott, Paul Moyer, Johnny Grant, Jonathan Winters, and Robert Easton. I thank them for their friendship and their contribution.

I first met my coauthor, Jeff Lenburg, in the early 1980s, and together with his twin brother, Greg, one of our great joint accomplishments was obtaining a star on the Hollywood Walk of Fame for the Three Stooges. Jeff has written books on the Stooges, Larry Gatlin, Dustin Hoffman, Veronica Lake, Steve Martin, and Dudley Moore. We've spent much time putting together this compendium and hope you find it not only enlightening and entertaining but also beneficial.

I plan to show you why a voice career is the most exciting thing since the invention of the Vort, a tiny machine enabling a person to send tapioca through telephone wires.

Well, I have to stop now. My chicken claw is breaking, and I've run out of butcher paper. I hope you enjoy the book!

Best krelbs always,
Gary Owens

Acknowledgments

WITH A CAREER as varied and successful as I have had, I have so many people I want to thank. They have enhanced my life over the years and have contributed to my success and, in some way, to this book.

To my fellow comrades in comedy, thanks for all the laughs. You lift my spirits with your humor.

From radio, a tip of the hat to the great talents with whom I have shared the airwaves. Special recognition to the talented writers and voice actors who have played an integral part in my radio shows and other areas of my career. Your gift for creative expression has made my work so enjoyable.

And special thanks to the many broadcasting executives who have been so good to me. You have hired me, honored me, and put up with me over the years. I salute you one and all.

My gratitude also to my fellow announcers, voice artists, and voice professionals. We share a love for verbal communication and understand that it is the "love of talk" that makes the world go round.

To the many fine actors, entertainers, and personalities I have known and worked with, you inspire me every day with your talent. To my friends in television and film who have been so supportive, my thanks. I owe much to the many wonderful producers and directors who have been so good to me—who hired me and taught me the trade.

To my fellow cartoonists and animation professionals, my deepest appreciation. Your talent is awesome. I am so honored to work alongside of you. To the many sports announcers, sports legends, players, coaches, and managers I have known, you are the greatest. Sports are a big part of my life, and I have enjoyed you all. My thanks to my agents for keeping me employed for many years. You've worked hard on my behalf, and I appreciate you.

A great deal of my continuing success goes to the many professionals in the media and related fields who have done such a wonderful job promoting me. I want to pay tribute to all the industry executives for your support as well.

My heartfelt gratitude to the legendary singers and songwriters and other music professionals I have worked with. Music makes the world a better place for all of us.

Certainly, I want to acknowledge the following groups for the use of sample scripted material in this book: ABC, CBS, Citron Haligman Bedecarre, Doner Advertising, Film Roman Productions, Fox, The Fuller Group, and Foote, Cone & Belding. Also Goodgoll Curtis Inc., George Schlatter—Ed Friendly Productions, The Martin Agency, NBC, Nelvana Company, TBS, United Cerebral Palsy, UPN, Warner Brothers TV, WTBS Superstation, and Western Images.

Thanks to Gary Amo, Army Archerd, Jim Bacon, Marilyn Beck, Jeanne Duvivier Brown, Adam Buckman, Wally Clark, Erica Farber, John Felz, Alice Germanetti, Kevin Gershan, Claude Hall, Dennis Holt, Rick Ludwin, Gary Lycan, Ray Richmond, Ron Rodriguez, Stacy Jenel Smith, Lee Solters, Stan Spero, Eliot and Bonnie Tiegel, and Ben Fong-Torres.

I also want to thank my family, who has always believed in me and encouraged me: my wife, Arleta; our sons, Scott and Chris; my sister Adeline Van Genderen; and our nieces and nephews, Ronnie, Bobby, Vikki, Gayle, Altman, Eric, Colin, Ashley, Kelsey, and Hannah.

Last, but certainly not least, very special thanks to our agent, Joelle Delbourgo, for selling this project; and to our editors, Denise Betts and Donya Dickerson, and to our project editor, Heidi Bresnahan, for believing in this book. And to Jeff Lenburg for his wonderful tenacity. He handled the stress of this project very well and never once mentioned the time I tried to make a phone call by dialing the microwave oven.

Your Voice Can Be Worth a Fortune

ANYONE WHO HAS ever been successful will tell you the first rule of success is, Don't tell everything you know. Well, I'm going to break that rule right now. I'm going to tell you everything I know about making a fortune with your voice . . . as soon as I can find a pen and write everything down. All set now. Here we go!

You wouldn't be normal if you didn't want to be successful at something, and if using your voice is what it takes, why not give it a try? There's money to be made with your voice if you know how to use it properly. Every day, at some point in time, at some place in the world, someone is using their voice and getting paid handsomely for it.

Just look around and see for yourself. Turn on your radio, and you'll hear a man, woman, or talking parrot selling some product or service that you wish you could have. Turn on your television, and you'll be greeted by a voice pitching any of a multitude of goods or products. Turn on your VCR, and you'll hear voices again—and that's *before* watching *The Sixth Sense*, starring Bruce Willis!

The people whose voices you hear are not those of creditors pounding on your door, wondering why you haven't made your last three Visa payments. No, but the people who own the voices you hear all have the same thing in common: They are making more money than they ever dreamed possible doing something they love, simply by using their voice.

Many years ago, only people with "star quality" voices could break into the business. That's no longer the case. Today almost any kind of voice is acceptable.

You don't have to do a variety of voices to be successful. It helps, but it's not necessary the way it once was. Some in the business succeed largely because they have mastered the art of creating many different kinds of voices and are always employed. But you can do just as well with one voice. The potential for success is great, and you can start yourself on your way to a challenging and exciting profession if you have determination, drive, and a little bit of know-how.

One of the best things about working as a voice artist is that you can work in many different industries and make yourself employable in all of them.

Radio offers tremendous potential for people who have a broadcast-quality voice and look good behind the microphone.

Radio offers tremendous potential for someone with a broadcast-quality voice as a news announcer, sports announcer, disc jockey, or talk show host. Top personalities in this area frequently make six and sometimes seven figures a year—that's hundreds of thousands to millions of dollars. Even if you don't reach that level, you can still earn a very good living. Depending on how high up the food chain you go and how many listeners you have, salaries can jump significantly, especially in the larger cities.

Similarly, opportunities abound in television as news anchors, weathercasters, sportscasters, and sports announcers, as well as doing play-by-play for various high school, college, and professional sports. Earnings for these television jobs are higher than in radio, higher in large markets than in small ones, and higher in commercial than in public broadcasting. Among television announcers, the news anchor's average salary is $65,000 a year, ranging from $25,000 in small markets to millions in the largest ones. Weathercasters' average salary is $55,000, ranging from $25,000 to millions. Sportscasters average $49,000 a year, ranging from $22,000 on up. And in all of these fields, individuals who reach "personality" status can earn a great deal more.

For example, as a sports announcer, once you become well known and established, you have the potential to make millions. Vin Scully, Al Michaels, Keith Jackson, Brent Musberger, Dick Enberg, the late Chick Hearn, and Howard Cosell are examples of great sports announcers whose folksy style connects with viewers while they are calling the action and who've made millions doing it.

You can also perform on-camera and off-camera work on network television shows and specials, working as a booth announcer doing station identification and public service announcements or promos plugging the latest shows. Promo announcers are paid on a per spot basis, and even doing a few assignments a week will add up, in terms of both compensation and experience. My late good friend and colleague Ernie Anderson made millions in this area. For many years, Ernie was the network promo announcer for ABC. He did all of the major promos for the network for nearly every movie-of-the-week, series, or special, except those I did when I was ABC's announcer for its "TGIF" (Thank God It's Friday) comedy lineup. Ernie was one of the top voices in the business. Ernie, Bob Ridgely, and I were voices for the network for many years.

With the right kind of voice or voices, you can make a nice niche for yourself doing commercial voice-overs. Those who do personality announcing, as I do, can enjoy great success in this medium. In Los Angeles, the rate of pay for doing commercials varies depending on whether it's for radio or television and whether you are doing off-camera voice-over work or on-camera announcing. The union rate for radio commercials is $350 per spot or more, plus 10 percent agent's fee, for thirteen weeks. If the spot runs longer, you're paid again.

While these fees may seem modest, once you start producing a high volume of work, the pay can be very lucrative. Doing a couple of radio or television commercials or promos a week, you can make literally thousands a month on top of whatever else you earn using your voice. This can translate into an additional six figures to several million in earnings each year, often for only a few days of work, depending, of course, on your notoriety and your name recognition in the business.

If you have a great natural speaking voice, you can also earn a living as a narrator. Narrators play an important role in film, television, audiobooks, and the home video industry, narrating works as varied as feature films, television programs, industrial films, home videos, and audiobooks.

The longer you work in this business, the more you find yourself in pretty select company and hoping that your tux still fits. Here, I'm with Robert W. Morgan, Ted Turner, Larry King, and Art Linkletter at a Hall of Fame induction.

Like television announcing, the earnings are based on a negotiated rate and can be a good source of income. The late Richard Kiley was one of the most successful narrators in the business. He narrated many, many documentaries.

Certainly, if you like doing character voices, then animated cartoons are another wonderful industry to which you can sell your talent. Some of the best and brightest names in the business have been successful because of their innate abilities to do many voices well.

If you do a variety of different voices, including different dialects, and producers are looking for specific "types" of voices, commercials can be worthwhile. Sometimes casting directors want a person with a Southern accent, or a New York accent, or an Irish brogue—and not somebody who can mimic these, but the real McCoy (and no relation to Walter Brennan).

Like actors in a major television series, voice-over artists are paid scale. Earnings can double, triple, or quadruple in time, since voice artists, like actors, earn residuals from every rebroadcast during the program's initial airing and after it goes into syndication. During one season, you can earn not only what you were paid to voice every episode, but also thousands, if not millions, more in residuals the same year. I was fortunate to be the announcer for the "Garfield and Friends" television series. The opening line has been used on every show for many years!

Obviously the earning potential is greater the longer the series is on the air. Take "The Simpsons," for example. Since debuting in 1989, it has become the longest-running prime-time animated series and has made multimillionaires of the actors who voice the characters. The voices behind America's favorite dysfunctional family—Nancy Cartwright (Bart), Dan Castellaneta (Homer), Julie Kavner (Marge), Yeardley Smith (Lisa), Hank Azaria (Moe, Apu, Chief Wiggum, et al.), and Harry Shearer (Ned Flanders, Burns, Smithers, Principal Skinner, et al.)—each received $1 million bonuses in 2001 and a big raise that did not cause anyone to "have a cow, man." They all were paid a record $100,000 an episode (or $2.2 million for a season of twenty-two episodes), increasing to $125,000 for the show's fifteenth season and now $250,000 per episode for the most current season. The series is still running in syndication. Who says there's no money in cartoons?

This was another wonderful moment, when I received my star on the Hollywood Walk of Fame (next to Walt Disney). Several thousand people were there to cheer me on. Pictured are (front row, left to right) Bill Welsh; my wife, Arleta; me; Jennilee Harrison of "Dallas"; William Hertz from the Hollywood Walk of Fame committee; (back row, left to right) Mel Blanc; Jonathan Winters; Mickey Mouse; and Tim and Daphne Reid of "WKRP in Cincinnati."

If you are not shy and love to be in front of an audience, public speaking is yet another avenue by which you can offer your services, serving as a master of ceremonies at a charity event or convention. After you become established, your earning power will increase. As an emcee, you can earn from $5,000 to $10,000 and up, or as a keynote speaker, $30,000 or more, for a single event. Before you know it, you can be making as much as six figures a year doing public speaking, in addition to other outlets, using your voice.

The Rewards Can Be Great

Like any career, working as a voice artist has its share of ups and downs but can be very rewarding. To demonstrate, here are my Top Five Reasons to Become a Voice Artist:

1. **You can be anonymous and famous at the same time.** Many voice artists are noted in the industry but unknown to the public.

2. **You can be any age.** A voice is a timeless property, unlike the Pet Rock or Nehru jacket, which went the way of the Edsel. (The what?)

3. **You can be either gender.** The voice-over business offers equal opportunities for men, women . . . even pet iguanas!

4. **You can be financially independent.** You may not own an island as Marlon Brando did, but you'll have fun and get paid for doing what you love.

5. **You can work flexible hours.** If you're a night owl or an early riser, you'll have plenty of opportunities to drum up and crank out your work.

Everybody Has to Start Somewhere

No matter what field of entertainment you decide to pursue, whether you hope to become the next Dan Castellaneta or Julie Kavner, the next Vin Scully or Don LaFontaine, or perhaps the next Gary Owens, you can expect a few disappointments in your quest to make your first million. It's all part of the business. Dan Castellaneta didn't make it overnight. Neither did Julie Kavner. But look at them today. They never gave up on themselves or their talents, and they are among the most powerful and richest people in the business.

So expect to have disappointments, but don't let them keep you from your goal. Here are five inherent disadvantages to remember in your pursuit of vocal riches:

1. **Building a voice-over career takes time.** Rome wasn't built in a day—actually it was built in 2,345 days—so don't expect to be a sudden, overnight success.

2. **Finding employment may be hazardous to your health.** Competition can be stiff, and you may have to be a waiter or waitress by night while pursuing your dream job by day. But don't feel bad. Everyone's been down the same path you have and had big holes in the soles of their shoes, too.

3. **Finding an agent is like sucking lemons.** It's not always easy. Many agents will listen to your demo and give your material the once-over—a once-over, perhaps, into the nearest trash bin. Although it may seem like it, it's not the end of the world. As some great sage once told me many years ago, "There's an agent for every talent and a talent for every agent." You could be next.

4. **Don't expect too much too soon.** Some people go into the business thinking they're going to be rich beyond belief the first year. That may well happen, but it's better to lower your expectations than to be disappointed and discouraged. Work at selling your voice because you love doing it, and the rest will fall into place as it should.

5. **Avoid overselling yourself.** Winning the See How Many Students You Can Stuff in a Phone Booth Contest in high school or the Greasing Female Channel Swimmers for the Olympics Contest won't cut it, but having a strong desire and a good voice will. Leave your accoutrements at home unless they're part of your act. Then, by all means, bring them.

I have received thousands of letters over the years from many actors, writers, disc jockeys, announcers, and wannabes of every kind and nature, all wanting to break into voice-over, all thirsting for success and to make their indelible mark in the business. A few years ago, I rediscovered one such letter. I was rifling through some old files in my office in Hollywood, and I came across a letter dated January 26, 1969. As I began reading it, I proclaimed, "Oh, my God!" The letter was from a college student from Ball State University in Muncie, Indiana, who used phrases like "hot diggity" to get my attention while seeking my advice. His name was David M. Letterman. Yes, the same David Letterman, obviously years before hosting the "Late Show" on CBS (formerly on NBC) and the evolution of "stupid pet tricks" on late-night television. The photo on page 10 shows a copy of that letter. I replied to David with the best advice that I could think of at the time, and it still applies today: "You really have to get an agent who believes in you." Apparently David took my advice, because he's now making zillions.

I use David as an example because it shows that everybody has to start somewhere. You may be the next David Letterman.

Strategies for Success

Breaking into the business with your voice involves strategy and preparation. It's like a coach preparing his team for the big football game the night before: If the team isn't well prepared, it has maybe a 50 percent chance of winning. (Unless, of course, your team has no talent. Then you might as well let the water boy coach the team for the rest of the season, while you take that vacation you always dreamed of in the Bahamas.) A 50 percent chance resulting from a 50 percent effort won't take you very far, but 100 percent effort will. Therefore, it's to your benefit to follow this simple strategy:

Be Unique

First and foremost, be unique. As agent Erik Seastrand of the William Morris Agency says, "The prospective talent must have an interesting

BALL STATE UNIVERSITY / MUNCIE, INDIANA 47306

THE CENTER FOR RADIO AND TELEVISION

David M. Letterman
2024 W. Main St.
Muncie, Indiana
January 26, 1969

Mr. Gary Owens
KMPC Los Angeles

Dear Mr. Owens:

    I am a senior in college and I have spent the last
three years in the field of commercial broadcasting, working
and studying. While I enjoy, and find challenge in
broadcasting,I have come to realize that is only because
it gives me an opportunity to use material which I have
written myself. I would enjoy a career in radio and
television only if it would involve creative writing;
more specifically, comedy.
    The problem is, however, that I don't know how
to get a job as a writer. I have had several occasions
to perform myy material successfully, but unfortunately
I don't pay myself to write jokes. When I graduate in
June, I have a job waiting in Indianapolis with the ABC
Television affiliate, where I have worked for the
last two summers as a booth announcer and weekend weatherman. "Hot Diggity", you may be saying to yourself by
now, but I would rather be a writer.
    As mentioned above, I am completely ignorant as
to what to do to prepare myself for a writing career,
or even what to do to secure one. If you have the
time, I would greatly appreciate any advice or suggestions
you could give. Thank you very much for yourtime and
trouble.

                              Sincerely,
                              David Letterman

You never know who may write to you for advice, but if they become famous, it becomes a great story to tell someday. That's true of this letter I received from a young college student named David Letterman.

sound. Will the public want to listen to this talent?" Your voice must offer a different quality, a different range, and be distinctively different from others. Don't copy other comics or voice artists if you want to be successful. Carve your own niche. Bring your own special brand of voices to the table, and serve them up. As some great sage, whose name escapes me, once said, "There's nothing better than the original." So is it with your voice.

John Wayne was one of the true American originals, and everyone in the world has imitated him. One of my biggest thrills was to be imitated by him on "Laugh-In." As the on-camera announcer I played on the show, I wore a 1940s-style pin-striped suit. When "the Duke" guest-starred on the show, they had a suit just like mine made for him. When he came out dressed like me, he said, in his usual big-man swagger, "Is it all right if I don't wear glasses?" I wore black-rimmed glasses at the time. I said, "It's OK with me, Duke." To which he replied, "I'm afraid no one will recognize me with glasses on."

Can you imagine not recognizing John Wayne? Even though John Wayne imitated me, he still wanted people to recognize him for who he was: a classic American original.

Be Real and Natural

Your voices, above all else, must sound real. Not like impressions of real voices, but as real as the people or sounds you are mimicking. There's no room for pale imitations. Sound as real as possible. Even when doing accents.

There's nothing wrong with voices that are different. As I stated earlier, this business has room for people with all types of voices. No matter where you come from, so long as you speak well and project your voice well, you can be tremendously successful in this business. You don't have to take diction lessons unless you want to. If you want to lose an accent or gain one, that's up to you. Having a different voice doesn't work against you the way it might have in the past. It used to be standard practice that your voice had to fit a certain style or mold. Not so today.

Back in the early days of television news, networks hired the Walter Cronkites and Chet Huntleys because their voices had basically no accents. Chet Huntley was from Montana, and Walter Cronkite was from Minnesota. Their voices were pretty clear, with no nuances of a Southern drawl or the nasal quality of the Bronx accent. For a long time, Peter Jennings of ABC News was the number one newscaster in America, and he's from Canada. Outside of an occasional "oot," he could be from the Midwest. Tom Brokaw from NBC News came from South Dakota; Dan Rather of CBS News from Texas, but you'd hardly know it. Today it doesn't matter where you hail from.

In addition to being real, voices should possess a natural quality (since everyone's voice is different, this is certainly possible). Kathleen Turner has a very sexy voice. Robin Williams can do many different voices and is funny doing them. Jane Seymour has a soft, sensuous voice. Dustin Hoffman has a deep voice with a natural quality. When you hear their voices, you know it's them. Their voices exude a familiar quality that is well loved, not only by the public, but also by advertisers.

Possess Self-Confidence and Perseverance

Confidence is very important. You must believe in yourself, because entering the entertainment business is like entering shark-infested waters. Many have been swallowed up and eaten because they lacked confidence.

To make it in this business, you must persevere no matter what obstacles you have to overcome. Fred Westbrook of Kazerian-Spencer says, "Tenacity, thick skin, and a good business acumen are important!" It is a competitive field, but the cream will definitely rise to the top. You must learn to accept rejection and not take it personally. Rejection is a great part of this business, no different than for any artist.

As the old saying goes, "For a man to truly understand rejection, he must first be ignored by a cat." This may not help if you are not a cat lover as I am, but the message is still a valid one. You'll need to learn to let any criticism bounce off of you, because in this field, at some time or another, you're going to be insulted and you're going to be degraded. The world of show business is full of naysayers, and nothing will ever change that. You will always come across people who will say, "This business is too hard. Look at the competition you have. Look at the percentage who make it." Let these barbs roll off your back like a wet noodle—macaroni, not spaghetti, since they usually stick—and don't take them personally. It's all part of the process. Think of the great success stories in our history. If those people had listened to others who tried to douse their dreams, some of the best and brightest ideas ever invented would never have blossomed.

Ray Kroc, the man who built McDonald's into a billion-dollar fast-food giant, was a friend of mine. A sign about perseverance he used to have posted in all of his McDonald's restaurants applies to what I'm saying. It reads, "Nothing in the world can take the place of perseverance. Talent will not; nothing is more common than unsuccessful men with talent. Genius will not; unrewarded genius is almost a proverb. Education will not; the world is full of educated derelicts. But perseverance and determination alone are omnipotent."

What this plaque states is certainly true. You may pick at random from a library shelf the biography of any man or woman who has made a lasting contribution to humanity. Some were extremely brilliant, others showed uncommon courage. But one characteristic will be present in every case. Every person who has achieved greatness has shown uncommon perseverance—and so must you.

One Success at a Time

My definition of success has changed through the years because every time I reached a new plateau in my life, the definition took on a new meaning. When I was a high school student, success was getting a job as an announcer. A short time later, that job proved to be a major stepping-stone to more success. I went from a small-market station to a bigger-market station, and so on. My idea of success changed with every new opportunity and kept changing every time I moved up or improved my current situation.

Confidence, perseverance, attitude, success, and many other square terms are all part and parcel of your ability not only to last in the business but also to succeed for many years to come. Well, enough of my Knute Rockne speech for now. It's time to turn the page—literally—or you won't read the next enlightening chapter in "the continuing saga about a poor rich girl . . . " (sorry, it's those bad habits again), I mean creating a classic voice that everybody will love and getting paid for it, too.

2

Creating a Classic Voice

YOU THINK YOU have a marketable voice. People have told you your whole life—or at least since yesterday—that you have a great-sounding voice, except when singing like Pavarotti in the shower. You've delighted friends with funny characterizations. You've even frightened away solicitors with your imitation of a pack of Goobers. These things take talent. So does creating a classic voice that will rocket you to success and keep you there.

How you arrive at the right-sounding voice takes hours of practice and patience. The good news, however, is that whether you want to be a disc jockey, newscaster, or announcer or to do commercials and cartoons, promos and narration, or public speaking and miscellany, the techniques you use to achieve success are all the same.

Find Your Voice

There are many ways to find your voice that don't involve going on a nationwide manhunt or enlisting hungry bloodhounds to sniff it out. First, find a voice—or voices—that fits you. Experiment with your voice until you find what works best for you. I know this all sounds too easy, but actually it is. The important thing here is to play around with your voice until you find a sound you like. Then work on perfecting your voice. There are many proven techniques that will help you achieve this, and I will discuss them later.

The quality of your voice is important, naturally, but so is belief in your talent. Not everyone will agree, even after you find the right voice, that you have the right stuff to make it in the business. People have been proven wrong.

Casey Kasem, best known to television viewers as the voice of Shaggy in "Scooby-Doo" and to radio listeners as the host of "American Top 40," faced this problem when he first tried breaking into the voice-over business. According to agent Don Pitts, when Casey arrived in Hollywood many years ago, there were only three voice-over agents in town.

Casey had an appointment with one of the three, a very distinguished gentleman named Bob Longnecker, who has since passed away. (Bob selected his clients by hearing them on the air.) After exchanging pleasantries, Casey asked where the microphone was in Longnecker's office. Bob said he didn't need a microphone to record anyone. He could tell by listening to him. A bewildered Casey was given a piece of copy and asked to read it from the other side of the room. After Casey read, Bob thanked him for reading and told him he should consider "a different career." He would never be a voice-over person. Of course, Casey went on to make many cartoons and commercials for top products in the country!

Recently, *Animation* magazine, for its fifteenth-anniversary issue, named the "fifteen top TV voice actors" of all time. Rounding out this prestigious list were Lucille Bliss, Daws Butler, Mel Blanc, June Foray, Stan Freberg, Paul Frees, Don Messick, Gary Owens, Bill Scott, John Stephenson, Jean VanderPyl, Janet Waldo, B. J. Ward, Frank Welker, and Paul Winchell. I'm so happy to have made that wonderful list. The artists who made it are icons in the business—deservedly so—and have become the standard by which great voices are measured.

Classic voices, one and all, they—and countless others, including such greats as Rob Paulsen, Billy West, Jess Harnell, Tom Kenny, Joan Gerber, Neil Ross, Greg Burson, Tress MacNeille, Jeff Bennet, Bob

Bergen, Greg Berger, and Kath Soucie—have literally transformed the profession not only through the quality of their voice but also through the quality of their work that people remember. That's why they are some of the most sought-after voices in the business.

Create a Classic Voice

"Why should I create my own classic voice?" you ask. Well, that's simple. By creating your own classic, you, too, will stand out in the crowd, be the toast of the town, be popular at parties, and someday make the Hall of Fame of Classic Voices, as the *Animation* magazine awards are called.

Creating a classic voice takes guts, determination, a strong will (even an ironclad one), the strength of a thousand horses (or a visit to the tomb of the unknown Clydesdales), but more importantly, it takes developing a voice that commands attention (and not just on street corners). How well you succeed will depend not only on the quality of your voice but also on the type of voice you do. The tremendous possibilities for using your voice include straight announcing, characterizations, impersonations, normal voices, and sounds.

Straight announcing basically involves doing one voice, that of an announcer or narrator. Many on radio or television—news reporters and actors—also do this kind of work. With a signature voice, you can land jobs in cartoons and commercials, as a booth announcer for a local television station or network, as an off-camera announcer on television programs and specials, and as a narrator for movies and audiobooks. For example, "You're watching 'Amazing Race' on CBS!" (My son Scott Owens is executive in charge of production for this Emmy Award–winning series.) Or Mason Adams, a fine actor who for many, many years has been the voice of Smuckers jelly: "With a name like Smuckers, it has to be good."

Voice acting involves doing cartoons and commercials. Some of the best talents in the business do a wide range of characters. Tracey Ullman is an example of someone who can play any role, and her English accent never becomes an issue in America because she has learned to drop it. On the other hand, some artists have been hugely successful doing the same characterization. Comedian Gilbert Gottfried is a very good example. Gilbert has made his living doing the same shrill voice in full-length animated features and cartoons for television. And he gets a king's ransom for doing the voice of the frustrated duck in the popular AFLAC commercials ("AF-LACCC!").

Impersonators who are primarily stand-up comics and actors, such as Rich Little, Robin Williams, Dana Carvey, and the cast of "Saturday Night Live," re-create existing and well-known people with their voices. Talented impersonators are valuable partners in all kinds of voice-over work, including narration, commercials, cartoons, television programs, and movies.

Normal voices are basically those that sound like regular people, such as the typical man on the street, a cop on the beat, a local farmer, a harried housewife, a guy at the hardware store, and people with accents.

Many people in the business make their entire living doing vocal sounds, such as birds, farm animals, monsters, and verbal magic for added effects in commercials and cartoons. Even in today's technological age, not everything you hear is computer generated. Many sounds are still done by live voice artists who specialize in doing various vocal effects.

The best way to develop a classic style is to listen to the remarkable talents who currently do commercials and cartoons. "Be obsessed with the craft of voice-over," says Paul Doherty, vice president of Cunningham-Escott-Dipene (CED), a leading Los Angeles talent agency. "Voice-over is about your point of view, your thinking and being, not just about your vocal instrument." Pay attention to the vocal characterizations. Keep up with trends and the kind of voices that are being cast. Don't copy from others, but develop your own style, your own personality. Record commercials, and write your own copy to practice—or use the sample scripts in this book. Try to capture the various qualities and moods in your way.

In developing your classic style, remember this—know the limits of your voice!

This reminds me of a funny story that Bill Scott, best known as the voice of Bullwinkle from the "Rocky and Bullwinkle" cartoon series, told me many years ago. Actor William Conrad was always complaining that he and Jay Ward, who created and produced "Rocky and Bullwinkle," never let him do anything other than his "narrator voice." (Conrad provided the narration for the "Rocky and Bullwinkle" cartoons and other Jay Ward hits: "And our pals Rocky and Bullwinkle are . . . .") The next time they needed an extra character voice, they told Conrad he could do it. He played a pygmy chieftain in one of the episodes, and he sounded exactly the same as he did as the narrator! What William didn't realize (and not even Jay Ward had the heart to tell him) was that his fantastic vocal talent had limits. But what a great narrator voice—one of the best ever!

One important rule is that you should always feel comfortable and natural with the voice you use and use only the voices you can do one hundred percent perfectly. Otherwise, you could strain and hurt your voice if you are not careful, as well as turn off your future employer.

When using your voice, you must know when to stop, when to rest your voice. Whatever you do, don't overdo it. Singer Johnny Mathis is a fanatic about taking care of his voice. He usually eats a little honey every day to soothe his vocal chords. So is actor Larry Hagman, of TV's "I Dream of Jeannie" and "Dallas" fame. One day a week, Hagman doesn't talk at all for the whole day to rest his voice.

While you probably won't need to go to these lengths, you should still treat your voice as the precious commodity it is. Preserve your voice when needed, especially if it's your only way of making a living.

The beauty about having a classic voice and being in the voice-over business is you never know who will call, or when, so you should always be ready.

One day, producer/director Blake Edwards called me and said, "I'm looking for someone for the voice of God." At first I thought Blake meant me because I've played God and I've played the devil. He said, "No, no. I want a female God." So I recommended several actresses who I thought could do the voice—Suzanne Pleshette, Brenda Vacarro, Colleen Dewhurst, and Linda Gary, who I think got the job. It just shows you never know when you will get called for something, even if it's to play God.

Develop Proper Vocal Techniques

My friend Robert Easton, Hollywood's "dialect doctor," has coached more than two thousand actors—Carol Burnett, Tom Cruise, Cameron Diaz,

Helen Hunt, Sir Anthony Hopkins, Demi Moore, Sir Laurence Olivier, Al Pacino, to name a few—to sound authentic doing some one hundred regional or foreign accents. Founder and president of the aptly named Henry Higgins of Hollywood, Easton, who, in his youth had a severe stutter, has parlayed his uncanny ear into a highly successful voice-coaching career. For over a half century, he has developed a unique method of speech training that involves many innovations—auditory, visual, and kinesthetic—that have earned his clients many nominations and awards, including Oscars, Emmys, Golden Globes, Screen Actors Guild awards, and Cannes Film Festival awards. To become more vocally versatile, create a wider range of character voices and accents, or develop that classic voice, Easton—a successful actor himself—recommends practicing the following specific methodologies that have worked for those he has tutored:

- Employ proper breath support for dynamic voice production without hoarseness, nasality, or stridency.

- Learn to use the resonating chambers in the upper and lower sinuses, the back of the mouth, and the chest to give color and richness to the voice.

- Control the vocal cords, the lips, and the tongue. (A one-millimeter movement in tongue position creates a perceptible difference in sound quality.)

- Understand the phonemic and allophonic sound systems of other dialects, including the particular sounds of standard American media-ese the other dialects lack and which sounds speakers of those other dialects may substitute for ours. (This awareness works equally well for those who wish to learn a dialect or lose one.)

- Vary the rhythm and intonation to avoid vocal monotony.

- Exercise different tone qualities to give the voice a range from the smooth texture of velvet to the rough texture of burlap.

- Make the voice match the looks for the role.

- Eliminate meaningless pauses, nervous air-gulping, and compulsive throat-clearing.

- Relax the jaws, tongue, and neck muscles to remove counterproductive tension in the voice.

- Use words and phrases as precision tools to express every subtle change in your thoughts and feelings.

Easton notes that many of these methods have worked like magic for people in other professions who wished to perfect their communication skills, including lawyers, business executives, magicians, members of the clergy, fund-raisers, doctors, and psychologists.

Another important technique is picturing the image you want to create. Consider the character you want to voice, and get inside it. Think, act, and become who or what you're trying to convey. Visualize and create with the inflection and nuances in your voice.

In the world of fashion, style is everything. The same is true with your voice. Producers like style as much as the substance of your voice, along with how creative you can be. As Kathy Lehman, a voice expert who heads an advanced workshop, once told me, "The people who seem to win and book spots are those who look at the copy and make the most out of it." She encourages her students and gives them "permission" to do what they will with the written word because that is what will get them the job.

Actor-comedian Tom Sharpe, a master of comedy improvisation who made a big name for himself in Detroit advertising speaking the term *Fahrvergnügung* for Volkswagen commercials, employs this same winning strategy. Tom looks at a script and asks himself, "What is the humor in it? What is the point I'd like to make?" That's what lights people up. Producers hire Tom because they are getting creativity beyond the voice. The same holds true for Joan Gerber, Julie Dees, and B. J. Ward, among the best who have landed countless jobs because of their improvisational skills.

Exude Personality

The most recognized individuals in the business today have one thing in common: personality. Having a good voice is not enough. Being able to read scripts is not enough. But doing both extremely well and exuding more personality with your voice will improve your chances of success. "Producers want to hear not only how you read the words, but how you apply them and the artistry with which you read," says agent Steve Tisherman.

As agent T. J. Escott notes, "Can the talent interpret the copy? And from there can they act out and tell the story that he/she has interpreted? The bottom line is can the talent effectively get his point across from the script so that the audience believes what they are being sold?"

Actors are often accused of overdramatizing their performances—of "overacting." Well, to exude more personality with your voice sometimes means doing just that. Play up the parts of your reading for effect. Project everything that goes into the character that you are reading but with more fervor, more feeling, and everything the script calls for—compassion, warmth, authority, respect, or humor—but in a *big* way with your voice. When my confrere Mel Blanc did the voice of Bugs Bunny idly chomping on a carrot and asking Elmer Fudd, "What's up, doc?" he played the part to the hilt. He exaggerated everything, from the ingratiating chomping of the carrot to Bugs's smart-alecky remark of "What's up, doc?" Mel's wonderful nuances and vocal quirks are what made Bugs Bunny one of the greatest cartoon personalities of all time. Incidentally, Mel was allergic to carrots!

Record Your Voice

The best method for evaluating your voice and characterizations is to commit them to tape. As a young boy, I used to listen to the great performances of Walter Winchell and Lowell Thomas. I tried to develop my own style. I would practice reading stories into my recorder at the kitchen table at breakfast, lunch, and dinner. My parents were naturally supportive. "Gary, put that down and eat your dinner." Well, most days they were. When recording your voice, focus on how you interpret and read dialogue, and try to be consistent in what you convey. To be effective, follow these six simple guidelines:

1. **Mind your microphone.** Don't sound as though you've just swallowed the microphone (although you should have someone who knows the Heimlich maneuver standing by just in case). Speak directly into the microphone, and project your voice with authority, keeping your mouth a short distance from the mike.

2. **Read the script over.** Familiarize yourself with the dialogue and what you're going to say. Practice until you feel you have the material—and how you want to say it—down pat.

3. **Analyze the script.** Understand what you are saying and what points you want to emphasize. I always underline key words that I want to emphasize, like <u>mercy me!</u>

4. **Watch your inflection.** Increase or decrease the loudness of your voice when necessary. Raise and lower your pitch, and create the right inflection. In other words, modulate the sound, choosing carefully when to do this so your voice is smooth and regulated and you properly emphasize what you're reading.

5. **Give thought to your transitions.** Think about when to change your tone at the end of the sentence or in the middle of one.

6. **Pace yourself.** As you read the copy, pace yourself. Don't rush. Pause while reading the copy. This will help you to attain a more natural sound in your voice.

The motto "Practice makes perfect" certainly rings true. Not everything you do will be perfect, but that shouldn't discourage you. The more you practice, the better you will sound, unless you have a delivery that

Courtesy: Fred Wostbrock.

Going "ape" over developing your voice isn't the answer if you want to make it in this business. But having a good voice and personality will help. Next door, the Quasimodo beauty contest took place, and the crowd turned ugly.

shatters windows. If something isn't working, then move on. That may not be right for you in the first place.

The point I'm trying to make is that it is important to work with your voice. Experiment with how you sound, and keep trying different voices until you find something that fits. When you do, stick to what works. Once you reach that point, the rest will fall into place.

Silly Yourself (I Beg Your Pardon)

One necessary component to any job is that you have fun with it, and one way to achieve that is to make humor and fun an essential part of your everyday life. The most successful people I have known have all possessed a finely tuned funny bone. So, when necessary, silly yourself ("Sorry, dear, I sillied myself"). Have fun with your voice, and make working with your voice a fun experience. From the sound of your voice, people can tell whether you're having fun or just going through the motions, which is lethal in this business.

It helps to view the world sideways, half-cocked and to be slightly absurd at all times. I've made my entire living this way. Anytime I find myself having an off day, I recall some of the weird and wonderful things done by famously successful people I've known. So if you are feeling a little discouraged, a little down, and a little blue in the face (exhaling will relieve that) at any point while launching your voice career or after coming in last in the triathlon, read the following silly-people stories. I guarantee these stories will cheer you up and put a smile on your face, and they beat hitting your finger with a hammer.

One time, I was having lunch with Peter Sellers and Spike Milligan at the famous Brown Derby restaurant. Bob Cobb said to us, "Have a seat." Spike said, "No thanks, I'm trying to cut down!"

Another time I lunched at the Brown Derby with my childhood idol Spike Jones, who didn't disappoint me. He wore a gorilla mask to lunch.

Pat McCormick is another wild and wonderful man. Pat always carried a little butter knife with him to restaurants. He would take the cold pats of butter and twang them against the beams of the ceiling right over the next booth. As the butter got warm, it started dripping on someone's head and would mess up the person's hair.

One of the great Hollywood stories is about Harry Crane, who was the head writer on "The Dean Martin Show." Harry was hypoglycemic and was in line for lunch at a famous deli in Los Angeles. He became very weak and rushed in front of twenty people to tell the host he needed a glass of orange juice and a peanut butter sandwich (for carbohydrates) right now!

The guy seating people, not knowing Harry had this problem, said, "You'll have to wait your turn, buddy. There are twenty people ahead of you."

Harry then passed out from low blood sugar and hit the floor. Paramedics were called, and he was taken to a hospital. The next day, Joey Bishop called him and said, "Harry, are you OK? What happened?"

Harry then explained. "I'm standing in line, and my blood sugar was dropping, and I go up front and tell the guy I need orange juice and a peanut butter sandwich. They tell me to get back in line, and I pass out. Then they bring me here!"

Joey says, "Geez, Harry, that's terrible. I wanna come visit you. What hospital are you in?"

Harry tells him.

Joey asks him, "What's the quickest way to get there?"

Crane says, "First, you go into the deli. Then wait in line. Order an orange juice and peanut butter sandwich. Then—"

Woody Allen was a guest on my radio show in the early 1960s. I've always loved his work—the more offbeat, the better. One of his greatest lines was "During a philosophy test in college, I copied from the soul of a student next to me!"

Phyllis Diller, one of the funniest comedians in show business, and I worked together on an episode of the Telepictures television series, "Street Smarts." Always quick with the funny quips and one-liners, Phyllis gave me this tip about having lunch at an unknown eatery: "When you point to a fly in your soup and the waiter addresses it by name, you should flee immediately!"

Paul Williams is one of my favorite pals, a great acting talent and a great singer-songwriter. His compositions have included "An Old Fashioned Love Song," "Rainy Days and Mondays," "We've Only Just Begun," "You and Me Against the World," "The Rainbow Connection," and "Evergreen," which he cowrote with Barbra Streisand. One time, Paul mentioned that, as a Boy Scout, he learned how to tie knots so well that one night he had to be cut out of his shoes!

Another reason I love him is that, when listening to the radio, he likes to call up Rush Limbaugh and request a song.

Of course, no discussion of silly people would be complete without Jonathan Winters. Jonathan and I have been friends for many years. He is the godfather of off-the-wall characters, all people he observed while growing up in Ohio. One day, Jonathan called me and asked if we could meet for lunch in lovely Toluca Lake, a tiny burb near beautiful downtown Burbank. I said, "Sure. Where?" He said at the Dana Drug Store not far from Pass Avenue. Johnny would meet me near the prescription counter.

Two older people were talking as I approached. The woman said, "I believe that's Jonathan Winters." The husband commented, "No. What would he be doing here? He'd have someone pick up his prescription."

As I neared the counter, I said, "Doctor, these two think you resemble Jonathan Winters."

The legendary funnyman said, "Well, doctor, a lot of people do that. I'm Doctor Lloyd Nurgler, and this is my coworker, Dr. Fendishman. Give them one of our cards."

I had no business cards on me. So I gave them one that just had been given to me. Jonathan said, "Our office is not far from here. We're open Monday through Friday from nine to five. But on Saturdays, I work with my brother-in-law. Your husband doesn't look well."

"I feel fine," said the querulous hubby.

"I've been telling him he should see a doctor," the lady said.

"Why don't you see me and my brother-in-law," Johnny said. "He's a taxidermist, and we'll stuff your husband and put little bunny eyes in him. He'll look better."

The husband and wife made a fast exit to the front door, and the husband was still haranguing his wife. "I told you that wasn't Jonathan Winters!"

3

Breaking into the Voice Biz

CONGRATULATIONS! YOU HAVE successfully completed the decathlon of training and education, and you've developed a marketable voice. Now you're ready for the big test.

No, you don't have to run a cross-country marathon on one foot or swim the English Channel with both fins tied behind your back. You won't have to climb Mount Everest or try your skill at skydiving without a parachute either. What you do have to do, however, is perhaps the most important step to achieving voice stardom: sell yourself.

By reading this far, you have shown me that you really want to become a successful voice artist. I am happy, delighted, even thrilled (please, pardon my lack of enthusiasm) that you have made it through the first two chapters. This shows me three things right away: first, you have a strong willingness to learn; second, you have a strong desire to succeed; and, third, you want to make a million dollars!

I promised you earlier in this book that I would lead you through the steps to launching a career as a voice artist. Well, I always keep my promise. I will dispense with the buffoonery and get serious for a moment to help you over the next hump and get you started on your journey to success.

By now, you've learned everything you will need to know about developing your own style of voice. The nuggets of wisdom you have learned, culled from my forty-odd-year career (*odd* is the operative word here), have doubtlessly pumped up your adrenaline, whetted your appetite, and made you hungry to explore what a career in the voice-over business can mean for you.

Well, get your explorer shoes on. It is time to get you on your road to riches. And to make that possible, you will need to acquire the tools of the trade. Naturally, I am referring to the best friends you will have in your career: your demo CD, résumé, and introductory letter.

Producing a Demo That Sells

You've spent most of your time mastering your voice or voices. Now it is time to sell others on your talent. There are several ways you can do this.

First, you could use the tried-and-true method of going door-to-door to plead with agents and producers to give you a chance. Most likely you wouldn't get in the front door or past the receptionist. Another method that has worked is to claim that you are their long lost cousin (nepotism never hurts, especially in show business). Then there is the traditional method that works almost every time: producing a demo.

A demo is what opens doors and sells your talents, and CDs are generally preferred these days. Yours should be cleverly produced and edited and feature only those samples that are strong enough to grab—and keep—the attention of agents, producers, and casting people. Producing a demo is essential; a demo is like your calling card. It is really the best way of introducing you and your talent to people in the industry. And it saves you the obvious embarrassment of taking desperate measures to be noticed—like eating a casaba melon without using your mouth.

The cost to produce a demo is moderate to expensive, starting at $100 and rising depending on the artwork, graphics, and any bells and whistles you add to your CD. Costs are likely to rise if you add sound effects, produce a high-gloss cover (with your photograph imprinted on the front), and choose pricier studio and duplication services.

As you do when buying a new car or furniture, you should shop around for the best price. Some recording studios offer group rates. This means that if you can guarantee the booking of several people who want to record their CDs, you can often get a special rate that is less than what you would pay to rent the studio yourself.

Keep It Short and Sweet

Every agent will tell you that the best CDs are short and sweet. Agents and casting directors are inundated with demos. They often receive hundreds of demos a month from beginning and established voice artists. It is your job to capture their attention as quickly as possible, to make them not only want to listen to your CD but also decide to represent you as their client.

The industry standard length for demos is two and one-half to three minutes. The only exceptions occur if you are trying to break into radio. Then your demo should be ten minutes—either an excerpt of a real broadcast, if you've worked at a college or commercial radio station, or if not, a made-up show with your own call letters, slogans, witty commentary, and bridges of music that you can shop directly to radio stations without an agent. For getting into television announcing, a five- to ten-minute video of your work will do the trick.

As my friend Steve Tisherman, one of the top voice agents in the business, tells me, "Nobody has time or the patience to listen to a demo that is long. The philosophy in my mind is 'Less is more.'"

I understand that three minutes does not seem like much time, but you would be surprised what you can do in those few minutes. You should spend only a few seconds on each voice, and the number of spots you record should correspond to the different characters you do well. One artist I know produced a demo that lasted two minutes yet, in that period of time, managed to put twenty-five different voices on it.

To work in commercials or animated cartoons, you will need to produce a separate demo for each. Your CD for radio and television commercials should contain examples of straight announcing as well as any characterizations you can do—a harassed husband or sugary-sweet housewife—and any other setups that fit into commercials and aren't too outrageous. On the other hand, your animated cartoon CD should feature character voices that work only in an animated setting (more about this in the animated cartoon chapter, Chapter 9).

In either case, make a demo that features a variety of different and entertaining voices. The characters that you do should be ones you can quickly and easily maintain on a CD, for an audition, or on the job.

If you don't possess a variety of voices and you can only do one or two characters but do them extremely well, then make a CD featuring those instead of padding your demo with others that are less than your best. You will find that it is better to do one or two minutes of what you do well—and impress your listeners—than to lose your audience by trying to oversell yourself.

Anyone who is producing a demo should concentrate on only those voices that they do best. Everything on the CD should be short and sweet, no more than fifteen to twenty seconds of any one voice. You're not there to sell me the product. You're there to show me a nuance of what you can do in a certain ilk.

Don't overextend your talent on your demo. If you don't do something well, don't put it on the CD.

Cathey Lizzio and Pat Brady of CED, who represent many of the best-known cartoon voices in the business, say, "We look for somebody with a unique sound in their voice. The mistake that most people make is everything on their demo has sameness about it. We receive demos all the time that have back-to-back commercials on them, but they all sound alike. If you don't give us something different, then we know what this person's act is, and there is no reason for us to listen any further. Range is what we look for."

Don Pitts suggests, "If you have just one voice, then give me some different attitudes. Different attitudes might be a tougher edge to your voice, perhaps for a truck or beer commercial. You might do something like a concerned-sounding voice—that of a parent. You could convey a business-sounding approach in your voice like a spokesperson for an insurance company or bank. Or maybe a soul-searching delivery trying to interest someone to enter an alcohol and drug rehab center. Now you have a person who has one voice, but he is giving you four different approaches using different attitudes."

Jack Angel, a veteran voice artist who provides his voice for commercials and animated cartoons, suggests that when making a demo, you record the first spot of the demo in your own voice. He says, "This answers the question agents and casting directors always ask: 'What does this person really sound like?' Once they have this point of reference, they are more apt to show interest in discovering your entire range of voices."

Please, Pass the Turnoffs

Anyone who is anyone in the voice-over business—even those who are someone—will tell you that some things can make your demo an instant candidate for America's Most *Un*wanted list.

Many of the industry's top agents, producers, and casting people have gone to considerable lengths—and heights—to compile for me their Top Ten list of demo turnoffs. Unfortunately, they could only come up with five, so you will have to imagine there are ten.

Here is what they recommend you avoid:

1. **Producing a demo that isn't your best effort.** "So many actors will send me demos, and they'll make excuses in their letter that it isn't their best," says Tisherman. "You are going to be thrown out to compete with the likes of yourself and others who are working a lot, so you better be able to compete."

2. **Doing more than you are capable of.** Jeff Danis, vice president of International Creative Management (ICM) in Beverly Hills, warns that newcomers and even those who are experienced, when making their demos, "should not try to be everything to somebody. Do what you do best. There are many people who have a tremendously successful career only doing one voice, but that's because they do it better than anybody else." Jeff represented me for fifteen years and is an integral part of the biz, and my career.

3. **Recording your demo prematurely.** Bob Lloyd, who headed The Voicecaster, a Los Angeles casting agency for voice artists that also conducts voice workshops, says, "I think a lot of people make demos before they are ready—before they have honed their skills to the point where they have a reasonable degree of competitiveness. They should wait until they

feel fully confident and ready. If I hear anything other than 'A' material, that usually turns me off."

4. Common-sounding voices. "If a woman starts her demo off with the voice of a wicked witch, I don't need to hear that," says Cathy Kalmenson, co-owner of Kalmenson & Kalmenson Voice Casting, a leading commercial audition company in Burbank, California. "Everybody does a wicked witch—even men."

5. Poor production values. Production values can often undermine the quality of your demo. Harvey Kalmenson, Cathy's husband and co-owner of Kalmenson & Kalmenson, says the overall sound of your demo should be a consideration when producing the demo to send to agents. As he says, "You are dealing with professionals, and the truth is, the sound quality of the demo is as important as your performance."

Choosing Your Material: Let Me Count the Ways

Producing a high-quality, memorable demo CD depends not only on how well you emphasize the points of your copy and on the quality of your voices but also on the material itself. You should select material that amounts to only a few lines for each character or voice that you plan to record. Then you will need to script the lines on paper—preferably typed and triple-spaced—so you can read the script without tripping up on your lines of dialogue. It should comprise material you have already prepared and practiced at home, or you can create all-new material for your demo from scratch. Whatever you do, practice the material several times before recording anything.

My suggestion is that you use what has been written and recorded by recognized radio and television advertisers who are selling products or services. Select only what best showcases your talents. When you are a beginner, I would not recommend writing your own copy, since good copy is not always easy to write.

To help you get started and demonstrate your range of voices on the demo, I have included actual scripts in upcoming chapters for your use for television announcing, commercials, and animated cartoons. Recording studios have sound effects libraries and can add background noises to your CD upon request.

Finding and Landing an Agent

Once you have successfully recorded your demo, you will be ready to get the show on the road—or, in this case, the CD in the mail to agents who will take notice of your talent and guide you down the path to success.

If you want to make it in the voice-over business, having an agent is an absolute necessity. It is almost impossible for any voice artist or actor to be noticed unless he or she has representation. Having representation is like having a life raft at sea; you can't possibly survive without it.

Agents are people in the know. They know what casting directors and producers like or want. They know how to sell your talent to people in the industry and arrange auditions for jobs that are best suited for your skills. They know how to negotiate the best terms for you once they have gotten you the job, and they know how to make the deal. In essence, agents are like three people working for you at once. They are your promoters. They are your business managers. They are your friends. Together, they can be your most valuable assets.

Producers and casting people also recognize how valuable agents can be. They turn to them to provide the best pool of talent for a certain property, whether it be a commercial or animated cartoon. The relationship that producers and casting people have with agents is simple. It is one of supply and demand. Producers and casting people call agents to supply them with a list of their best talent to audition for a specific part. They select some talent, reject others, and develop their own preferences for the voice artists they would like to audition. It is the agent's job to call in the clients the agent feels are right for the part and to record each of them reading the same spot. Afterward, the agent sends the demos to the producers or casting people for them to select the artists they would like to test for the part.

Some agents will produce what are known as master reels. This is the talent agency's demo featuring spots of several artists from the agency's voice-over roster. The spots are usually separated into groups (male and female), and each spot is preceded by the artist's name. Agents will send the CD to casting people all over the world. This showcases your talent in front of those who may need your type of voice in the future. Don't be surprised if your agent charges you for this service. Most agencies will charge you a minimal fee—usually several hundred dollars—to cover their production costs.

If there is anything you should know about agents, it is these three points:

1. Agents would like nothing better than to find someone who can make them money.
2. Agents want to raise their standard of living just as much as you do. (You want to rent a better apartment; they want to buy a Bel Air mansion.)
3. An agent makes money only when you work. (He or she earns a flat 10 percent of your gross paycheck; you pay more taxes to the IRS.)

When you take all these points into account, you really have a win-win situation.

There are at least three ways that, with some effort, you can find an agent. The first is through a friend already established in the business who can set you up with his or her agent (some agents prefer referrals). A second way is to have an agent watch you work. Most legitimate voice workshops have what they call "agents' night" as one of the classes. Students are given the opportunity to perform before agents in the business. The third way is to do what most actors and actresses who are now in the business did in the beginning—that is, consult your local phone book and entertainment directories or weekly trade papers (*Hollywood Reporter* and *Variety*) for agencies, large or small, that have a voice-over division or specialize in handling voice-over talent. Dave Sebastian Williams's *The Voice Over Resource Guide* is great, too. It lists agents, recording studios, and more.

Using the directory listings, you should develop a list of names, addresses, and telephone numbers of all agents franchised by the Screen Actors Guild (SAG) and the American Federation of Television and Radio Artists (AFTRA) whom you want to contact. While it's generally true that most agents are in New York and Los Angeles, there are actually agents all over the United States to act as your representative (see the back of this book for a partial list of agents). AFTRA (aftra.org) represents its eighty thousand members in four major areas: news and broadcasting, entertainment programming, the recording business, commercials and non-broadcast, and educational media.

In selecting an agent, don't start at the top—especially if you suffer from acrophobia. Bigger agencies don't mean better service. In most cases, they are too busy to give you the time and attention you need if you are a beginner. Contacting a medium-sized or smaller agency has its advantages. You can determine the size of an agency by checking the trade directory listings. Usually the entries list how many agents work at a particular agency. These agencies will be generally more receptive to hearing from you. The agents of these firms are more likely to consider and screen new talent, since they want to be successful, and discovering new talent can be a good way. They'll give you more attention than a bigger agency will. They'll also promote you more and in the long run be as effective.

Various talent agencies throughout the United States and around the world represent voice-over talent. The agencies are too numerous to list them all. However, one of the best places for finding talent agencies on the Web is Voicebank.net.

This one-stop resource covers all aspects of the voice-over business, from showcasing talent to connecting you to advertising agencies, talent agencies, casting directors, production houses, and more. One of the best features of Voicebank.net is its large online database listing dozens of national and international talent agencies. Listings include important contact information, where available, including address, phone and fax numbers, and e-mail and Web addresses.

Logging onto the Voicebank.net site requires a user ID and password. Membership is free. To join, simply complete the online membership form, including your desired log-in name and password and your name, e-mail address, and phone number.

Your First Mailing

Once you've compiled your list, it's time to plan your first mailing. Surely, you are enthusiastic and want to share your demo with as many agents as possible. Your natural tendency will be to send your demo to every pro-spective agent at once. This can be both time-consuming and expensive, and your postal carrier will hate you forever.

I recommend sending CDs to a select number of agents to start with—at least five agents simultaneously—and reevaluating your plan as you go along. You will find this conservative approach more to your liking —and your pocketbook—until you land an agent and, of course, your first job.

Before mailing your CDs, make preliminary phone calls to the agents on your list. Some agents may not be accepting new clients, so by calling them first, you can pare down your list to agents who are worth your time and the cost of a CD.

When calling, ask the receptionist for the agent who represents voice-over talent, and then ask to speak to that agent. Whether you speak to the agent or the agent's secretary, keep your conversation courteous and professional at all times.

Identify your reason for calling ("Hi, my name is Ima Beginner, and I am seeking representation . . ."), and ask if you may send in your demo. The receptionist or agent may tell you that they are not accepting any more voice-over people at this time. If this is the case, make a note to check back with them in a couple of months, and assuming you haven't found an agent by then, keep calling the others on your list until you strike pay dirt or a reasonable facsimile.

When an agent expresses interest in reviewing your CD, double-check the spelling of the agent's name and the complete mailing address of the agency before mailing your demo. Nothing will offend an agent more than if their last name is Young and you've spelled it as Hershkowitz.

Most agents will accept a CD to listen to. Always send a copy of your CD, and mail it in a padded envelope so nothing arrives folded, spindled, or mutilated. Never mail your master. Keep your master stored in a cool place, such as a closet, file cabinet, or refrigerator.

Above all else, your package should look professional and be pre-sented to an agent in a totally professional manner. Before mailing your demo, you will need to include a typed résumé and personalized letter to the agent. Your letter should be professional and to the point. Avoid writ-ing letters that are too cute, sound like you're pen pals, or are the length of the novel *War and Peace*. Remember your audience. These are busi-nesspeople you are contacting, so you want to make a favorable impres-sion. Your letter will tell everything about you—the good, the bad, and the ugly. So it is essential that it be well written and to the point.

The following examples are good approaches for cover letters and résumés you can use to accompany your demo. The first résumé is an example of one for a beginner who has no representation. The second sample is for someone with more professional experience.

Once you have drafted your cover letter and résumé, you'll package your CD and mail it promptly. After a reasonable amount of time—at least three days after you've mailed your CD—you should follow up on your mailing with a pleasant telephone call to the agent to see if your package arrived. The best times to call agents are between 10 A.M. and 2 P.M., Mon-day through Friday. Afternoons on Fridays are generally the busiest for agents, so this is not the best time to try calling them.

Your phone call will usually be handled by the agent's secretary. When calling, act friendly and courteous at all times. State your reason for calling ("I mailed a demo early this week . . . ") and that you want to speak to the agent ("I'd like to speak to Wanda B. Starr, please").

Your conversation may end up going one of three ways: The secre-tary will hang up, tell you to call back, or ask you to set up an appoint-ment. If they hang up, try again some other time. If they suggest y ou call back, log the information for a future call. If they ask you to set up an appointment, put the champagne on ice, and don't spare the glasses.

Some agents will respond more quickly than others. If an agent has listened to your demo but informs you that he or she is not interested, there can be several reasons:

- The agency may already represent a client whose voice or reper-toire of voices sounds like yours, so this would create a conflict of interest.

- The agent may be interested in talent with more range than you have demonstrated on your demo.

- They're just not interested.

Your name
Your street address
Your city, state, zip code
Your telephone number

Today's date

Mr. Michael Nurgleman
The Nurgleman Agency
3000 Nurgle Way
Los Angeles, California 90028

Dear Mr. Nurgleman:

I am a voice-over artist, and I am seeking representation. I perform both straight and character voices, and have enclosed a copy of my demo for your consideration.

I believe that I am a perfect candidate for representation. I am the top-rated morning DJ at Power 101 FM, the most-listened-to rock station in my area. I have been doing professional voice-over work for three years. I do a wide range of voices, from straight announcing to character voices. Recently, I completed several new radio commercials and narrated an independently produced animated cartoon short that will debut this January at the Palm Springs Film Festival. I am including these in the attached demo.

I have enclosed a self-addressed, stamped envelope for your convenience in returning the demo. Thank you for your time and your consideration. If you have any questions, I may be reached by phone at [your daytime phone number].

Sincerely,

Dee Dee F'nork

Remember, no matter what an agent tells you, it's not the final word. Sooner or later, there will be an agent who will recognize your talent. And when that happens, you'll feel like Jimmy Cagney in the closing moments of the movie *White Heat*. You'll be "on top of the world, Ma."

Your name
Your street address
Your city, state, zip code
Your telephone number

Today's date

Mr. Michael Nurgleman
The Nurgleman Agency
3000 Nurgle Way
Los Angeles, California 90028

Dear Mr. Nurgleman:

Thank you for taking time to talk to me about your interest in reviewing my demo.

As I mentioned, I perform a wide range of voices—straight announcing and character voices—and believe I can apply myself in several fields. I have been doing professional voice-over work for three years. Recently, I made a demo of several new radio commercials and a narration of an independently produced animated cartoon short that will debut this January at the Palm Springs Film Festival.

I have enclosed a copy of my demo, plus a self-addressed, stamped envelope for your convenience in returning the demo.

I look forward to talking to you again in the future. If you have any questions, I can be reached by phone at [your daytime phone number].

Again, thank you for your interest.

Sincerely,

Dee Dee F'nork

Meeting with Your Prospective Agent

You're about to meet an agent for the first time. You don't know what to expect. Your hands feel cold and clammy. Your heart is beating so loud it sounds like a marching band. You have this lump in your throat, and you

IMA BEGINNER
3650 Poltergeist Lane
Goobley, Idaho
(717) 555-5959

COMMERCIALS
• Mother Susie's Boutiques, Cable TV

OTHER EXPERIENCE
• Radio Announcer, Goobley University Radio Station
• Public Service Announcer, Goobley University Radio Station

TRAINING
• Voicepeople Workshop
• Public Speaking and Debate, Lenimore High School

CHARACTERS
• Mother
• Friendly Next-Door Neighbor
• Child (4–5 years old)
• Child (9–10 years old)
• Belligerent Policewoman
• Shy Teenager

IMPRESSIONS
• Whoopi Goldberg
• Goldie Hawn
• Roseanne
• Kathleen Turner
• Wallace Beery

ACCENTS
• Bronx
• Cockney

discover it's not your Adam's apple. You have butterflies in your stomach. (I once interviewed a butterfly, and he had an actor in his stomach.) And you haven't even pulled out of the driveway.

This is nothing more than a case of show business jitters. Every entertainer gets them. It's only natural. Meeting your first agent can cause that same feeling of uneasiness, nervousness, and eagerness.

DEE DEE F'NORK
CONTACT: Lyle Agent
Fly-by-Night Voice-Over Agency
Phone: (213) 555-7777
SAG, AFTRA

SUMMARY
Professional and experienced voice artist offers a wide range of services. Known for innovative achievements in national and locally broadcast radio and television commercials and animated cartoons. Highly skilled in on-camera and off-camera voice-overs, narration, character voices, and a variety of dialects.

CURRENT COMMERCIAL AND PROFESSIONAL EXPERIENCE
• Pets "R" Us (Local Radio)
• Mamma Mia's Pizza (Network Television)
• Hi Pro Dog Food (National Radio)
• Mr. Jim's For Tall & Big Men (Network Television)

CURRENT ANIMATION EXPERIENCE
• Witch Is Witch, Gem of a Jam (Toddle Tales)
• Lend a Paw, Missing Links (Petey the Pup)
• Pack & Unpack, Double Trouble (The Ant Hill Mob)

ACCENTS INCLUDE
• Brooklyn
• Russian
• French-Canadian
• Australian

You shouldn't be worried, however. When agents meet with you, it's because they heard something on your demo that made them think they could sell your voice. Agents don't bite, and most of them are warm and friendly people. They want to make you a star and an honest buck, so you wouldn't be sitting there waiting at their agency if they didn't feel you had what it takes to be a successful voice artist.

You will save yourself misery and bottles of Maalox by going to your interview prepared. You should take several copies of your résumé and demo along with you. This is in case the agent wants to show them to other people at the agency. Also, you should develop a list of questions in your mind that you would like to ask the agent, like "Where do I sign?" and "When will I make my first million?"

During your interview, there are several ways you can win an agent over. You can use charm, gentle persuasion, and secret payoffs, but nothing will make your interview more successful, from start to finish, than to follow these Seven Golden Rules:

1. **Be on time.** Every good excuse has been used already, so if you're late, at least come up with something original. "My pet yak bit me" has always worked.

2. **Be warm and friendly**—even if your car was just totaled.

3. **Dress comfortably, and wear clothes that look good.** When you wear a tie, always wear a shirt with it. And avoid using the word *rad* a lot.

4. **Keep everything positive during the interview.** Drop the fact that you were arrested for smoking a snow tire or that divine guidance comes from watching Hugh O'Brian movies.

5. **Let the agent do most of the talking**—even if it's true that you enjoy removing icicles from the nostrils of the presidents at Mount Rushmore in the winter.

6. **Relax, relax, relax.** Non-stress yourself!

7. **Be yourself.** And mention that you give generously to many causes, including the Bel Air Slighted Child Fund.

At some point during the interview, the agent may question you regarding your background and personal goals, and even put you to work reading copy. To impress the agent, be as obliging as you can. But, when necessary, also exercise your Fifth Amendment right. An agent doesn't need to know that you once removed all your clothing while standing on a table in a cafeteria or that you feel that Anna Nicole Smith is following you around town, driving a power lawn mower. None of this will ensure representation.

Don't think that just because you have a great-sounding voice and the agent is interested in you that you can be picky. Be willing to take whatever jobs are offered to establish and make a name for yourself. Getting established as a dependable voice-over actor is important. The more jobs you do will build your stature in the biz.

Talented voice agent Jeff Danis was representing Meryl Streep in the voice-over and commercial area a few years ago. One day, a young and inexperienced producer from a top ad agency called him about Ms. Streep. The producer asked Jeff if he could send Ms. Streep's voice-over demo to her office. Jeff explained to her that Ms. Streep did not have a voice-over demo. She is world famous, and everyone knows what she sounds like. With great agitation, the producer explained that her client wanted to hear Ms. Streep's voice. Jeff reiterated that her request was just not possible. The young producer persisted, and in exasperation, Jeff suggested that if the client really wanted to hear the actress's voice, he or she should rent one of Ms. Streep's movies.

"No," the producer said, "that would not work . . . they all have accents."

When You've Landed an Agent

Certainly the service provided by your agent is not free. Once agents secure work for you, they expect to receive their commissions in return for their good-faith effort in landing you that plum assignment as that man cavorting around as a human grape in the next Fruit of the Loom commercial.

There is always one client who isn't interested in paying commissions. Orson Welles was very good at that. He felt it was an "honor" for agents to "know him." His agent, Don Pitts, never quite looked at it that way. He expected Orson's commissions as much as anybody else's.

Anytime Don got Orson a job, Orson would suggest it would be easier to have all checks sent to *him*. (In other words, bye-bye commission.) By accident, Don got a call one day from a young woman who said she was "Mr. Welles's bookkeeper." She wanted some information about a job that Orson had done. Don told the woman everything she needed. The woman said how busy Mr. Welles was and that she didn't have time for details. Don told the woman that Orson sometimes forgot to forward his commissions to him and that he would be "happy to come by her home to pick up" the checks.

"Oh," the woman said, surprised, not knowing what else to say. "That would be fine." Problem solved.

From the start of your working relationship, you should impress upon your agent that you will be available when called, any day, any night, any time of the day. That the person on the demo—and that he or she is meeting with—is really you. And that you are alive, not dead.

Nobody understands this better than Jeff Danis, who formerly represented the estate of Elvis Presley for commercial endorsements. One day, a young producer called him to ask about the possibility of using Mr. Presley in a commercial. Jeff explained to him that the estate was very careful to protect his image and that he would have to know more about the product before he could agree to any association.

The young producer said he would be happy to give more details once he spoke to Mr. Presley himself to see if he was interested. In disbelief, Jeff calmly explained to the producer that obviously he dealt with the estate, not Mr. Presley, since the singer was dead.

"Really," the producer queried. "When did he die?"

By following these simple steps, you can rest assured that you will pass the ultimate test. By the end of the interview or the following day, the agent will inform you that he or she wants to act as your representative. After you have picked yourself up off the floor, you will be ready for your next and final hurdle: the audition.

Auditioning for Your First Job

Your chance to be a vital, creative component in many different areas of the entertainment business and enjoy the sheer pleasure and satisfaction of using your voice has finally arrived. You've waited in breathless anticipation for that call from your agent, and he's finally scheduled you for your first audition. Now what?

I remember my first audition. I was so determined to make something of myself that not even wild geckos could have stopped me. I didn't get the job, but I learned a very important lesson: Auditions are like shopping for a used car; there are always a few lemons in the bunch. Just make sure you're not one of them.

During an audition, you may find that someone does a voice that sounds like yours—even better. Competition will be heavy, and your percentage for success will not always be high. But it's important not to lose sight of your talent, your goals, and the chance to strive for riches. When it comes to auditions, over the years, I have followed the following Five Rules of Thumb—or Thumbs to Rule By:

1. Don't just be on time, be early. As my friend and agent Peter Verano has said, "No matter how long you are in the business, the extra time to settle down and prepare will always give you an edge over the competition."

2. Don't complain about the copy. No matter how poorly you think the copy has been written or how little you care for that particular brand, your job is to make it work. If you won't, there are others who will.

3. Don't waste your energy. Don't waste time at auditions on needless conversation and routines with other performers, like "You're only young once, but you can stay immature indefinitely." Forget about what's going on around you, and put all your energy into your audition. "Take that time to get focused," says Andrea Romano, cartoon casting director at Warner Brothers. "You are there to work, not socialize."

4. Be true to yourself. Don't try to sound like the flavor of the week. Be true to yourself. Remember, you do yourself better than anyone else can. You made it to this point for a reason—and not just because you actually "read" the directions to get there: Someone sees the talent in you. Follow your instincts.

5. Give that little extra. Voice coach Susan Blu suggests that when you are reading for a job, it's that little extra that counts. Often with her students, when they are doing a cold read, she'll say to them, "How about one more for the hell of it." Inevitably, she says, that is often the very best read. It's the "for the helluva it, see what hits me" read that leaves the best impression because the students have permission to make it instead of listening to themselves and worrying.

At an audition, you never know who will be watching your performance. There could be a casting assistant, a director, producer, or any number of important people who are involved in the decision-making process.

When it's time for you to audition, don't worry if the producer, casting director, and whoever else is in the room don't have a big smile on their face when you walk in (especially the casting director, whom you tried tipping). They've probably already seen hundreds of people, so be professional and give them what they want.

Typically, at auditions, they may ask you a few questions before you get started. Some of the most frequently asked questions are "Where are you from?" "How old are you?" and "Do you kiss on the first date?" Just be yourself. Be enthusiastic. Stay and act positive throughout the entire process. Your real challenge will come when they ask you to do a cold reading of the script to see you in action—a true test of your ability under pressure.

The best way to impress casting people when doing your reading is to care about what you are reading and act it. Vividly imagine what you are reading, and make everything else in the room disappear in your mind. It's just the script and you. Wow them with every word, every nuance, every inflection in your voice, but be careful not to overdo it. Keep them engaged in your performance, and keep doing this until you've finished. When it's all over, thank everyone for giving you the opportunity to audition.

After narrowing down the best candidates, usually they will have callbacks, which means you did something right to catch their attention. At a callback, there may be more people in the room than at your first audition—the writer, the producer, the director, the assistants, and the clients themselves. Callbacks are more personal than your first audition; they generally try to become more familiar with you and get to know you better.

Winning your audition is like playing a game of poker: Sometimes it's the luck of the draw. Sometimes it's just not your day. Sometimes it's not even the right audition. You turned left instead of right and wound up at the Save the Charmin Convention. Not getting the job is not necessarily because you lack talent.

Half the time, most producers don't even know why they turn down certain talent. They generally have nice ways of letting you down, although the reasons for rejecting your talents can often come across as cold and unoriginal. The three most common examples I can think of are:

1. "Sorry, you don't *fit* into our plans." (Translation: We couldn't think of a reason that sounded good.)
2. "Your voice isn't quite what we were looking for."
3. "You are too tall for this spot, but we'll call you next time."

No matter what reason they give you, it doesn't mean they are always right. The people who make decisions have been wrong before, and they will be wrong again. As Mark Twain, everybody's Huckleberry friend, once commented, "Let us be thankful for the fools. But for them the rest of us could not succeed." Whatever happens, don't be discouraged. Better days are ahead.

I believe it was Alfred E. Smith—or maybe it was Alfred E. Neuman?—who said, "No matter how thin you slice it, it's still baloney." I'm not sure how this famous quotation relates to auditioning, but I'm sure there is a much deeper meaning here.

4

Jockeying Your Way to Stardom

YOU HAVE MANY career options for using your voice to achieve your goal of earning millions. We've discussed a few of them at various lengths, and you may be beginning to feel like you're the lucky contestant on a game show, presented with several enticing options and not knowing which is the best one to choose. Behind Door Number One is a lucrative career as a radio disc jockey; Door Number Two, a fantastic career as a news announcer; and Door Number Three, someone who sells you a deed to a Talcum Powder Ranch!

Ah, you picked Door Number One. Unlike the guy next to you, who thought Door Number Three was a real steal, you've made a wise and wonderful choice. So a career in radio is for you? Well, you've come to the right place. I can think of no greater vocation or profession that will provide such excitement and pleasure throughout your life. In this chapter, I'll give you the lowdown—and then some—on everything I know about becoming a major on-air personality, and in no time flat, you'll have radio stations around the world begging for your services. At the very least, you'll get a call from a small station in Malta.

Radio is a good choice for many reasons. Because radio stations operate twenty-four hours a day, you can work at any time of day or night, allowing you to explore even more opportunities with your voice when you're not on air. You may work through the middle of the night, at the crack of dawn, or on a regular day shift. This can be advantageous to your career. During your off time, you can pursue other avenues with your voice and your goal of millions. Few jobs in the world offer that kind of flexibility.

Disc jockeying is an exciting and fun profession. You play a few records. Read some commercials. Throttle your station manager. Actually, disc jockeys do more than play records and make witty remarks. Sometimes they have to be a DJ, production manager, public relations promoter, account executive, and news reporter all in one.

Much has changed in radio since I first broke into the business. I've seen the aging of rock stars. (Today when you hear, "Ladies and gentlemen, the Stones are coming," be careful; it may not be a band!) Yes, it's all changed. When I started in radio, the world was a different place than it is today. When teenagers brought 45s to school, they were records, not guns. The most popular Stern on radio was Bill, not Howard. If you saw a Bronco being chased on the screen, it was by Gene Autry through a gulch, not by police down a freeway! But, through the years—all the culture changes, all the format changes—I've loved every minute of my time working in radio.

To become a major force on radio, this chapter describes what I call the Gary Owens Twelve Steps to Superstardom, Success, and Other Big Words Starting with the Letter S, not to be confused with any other twelve-step programs. If you are trying to kick some nasty habit, this program may not help you. Obviously, if you have no other place to go and your support group is out of town for the weekend, you're welcome to sit in anyway. Simply follow each step, and you, too, will be able to write your own book someday. Ready? OK, here we go!

Step 1: Educate Yourself

A college education is always an asset but isn't essential to work as a radio disc jockey if you have a broad base of knowledge. It depends on the kind of radio show you want to do.

You can manage with a radio or broadcasting trade school education, provided either that your other knowledge is inherent to you or that you are a voracious reader. Many people in the entertainment business have never finished college. Many of them went one or two years but never earned a bachelor's degree or completed extensive higher education. That said, competition for radio jobs is keen, so an education *is important*. Completion of a community college program or trade school will be an asset. Incidentally, when I first met NY radio great Don Imus, he was attending the Don Martin School of Broadcasting in Hollywood.

Radio and broadcasting schools are fine if you make the most of them. They teach you the basics—how to run the equipment, how to stand in front of the microphone, how to project your voice, whether you are popping your *p*s, how to turn the microphone in a certain direction, and so on.

The important thing in furthering your education is being able to hone your craft. After graduating from high school, I attended Dakota Wesleyan University in Mitchell, South Dakota, a small liberal arts college, not far from where I grew up. Former presidential candidate George McGovern was my history teacher, and Joe Robbie, who later owned the Miami Dolphins, was my economics professor. It was a good school for one-on-one learning and was overall a worthwhile investment of my time and money.

I worked my education around other jobs in related fields so I could gain practical experience at the same time. I held down two full-time jobs and went to college full-time so I could develop a résumé of material that I could later show to prospective employers. I attended classes from eight in the morning until noon. Then, at 12:30 I went on the air at KORN, where I worked as a newscaster, and did my first newscast of the day. After my last newscast at 10:30 at night, I would run across the street and write sports and editorials or draw cartoons for the *Daily Republic* newspaper. I wrote for a fellow South Dakotan, the genius Al Neuharth, the founder of *USA Today* and CEO for the Gannett Company. Al also published a weekly paper called *SoDak Sports* (South Dakota Sports). I was a writer for that, too. In the end, all of the hard work and effort were worth it. Al is one of the foremost names in journalism and publishing.

Ray Bradbury, another dear friend of mine, said the way a person becomes a great writer is by simply writing every day. It's the same with being a disc jockey. You become good simply by doing it every day, by doing it all the time.

Step 2: Start Small, Dream Big

To break into the business, you're better off starting small and dreaming big than starting big and dreaming small. In a short time (or as fast as the sand in the hourglass emptied, whichever came first), I went from working for a 250-watt station to several of the most powerful stations in the world.

When you feel you are ready, start your career in a smaller city. Give yourself two to four years to develop your craft. This is especially important if you don't attend college or complete some form of higher education. The equivalency would be spending as many years as you would in a place of learning. You master doing everything—announce sports, report

Courtesy: Fred Wostbrock.

"Start small, dream big" is my philosophy when it comes to having a radio career. So are having a pot of freshly brewed coffee on hand—in case you have to pull an all-nighter—and making the coffee nervous.

the weather, impart the news, serve as disc jockey—and you become a jack-of-all-trades in the process.

Starting in a small town is good because you can learn your craft without a million people hearing your mistakes. (The same applies if you want to become a news announcer or sports announcer.) This will give you time to get all of the flubs, awkwardness, uneasiness, and goop out of your system before moving on and up. If you are not ready, working for a major-market radio station can be pretty unrelenting. If you goof up at a small station, you can recover and learn from the experience. But in the bigger markets, there's little tolerance for error.

I learned this lesson the hard way when I became a disc jockey strictly by accident. I was working as a newscaster at the time at beautiful KOIL in Omaha, and the morning man couldn't stand the owner of the station, a man named Don Burden, who went on to own the entire chain of Star Stations. The two of them were like oil and water; they didn't mix. In the middle of the show one day, the DJ got mad at Don, cursed him on the air, and quit. I had to take over his show because I was the only one there. The program director, in a panic, said, "Gary, can you take over? You know how to run these turntables, don't you?"

Well, what else could I say? I said, "Oh, sure." I had never run a turntable in my life.

There were six turntables, three on each side, a lavalier microphone, and two Magnacorder recorders. Naturally, because of my lack of experience, I goosed everything (with apologies to Mother Goose). I was just terrible. I thought, "Oh, God, my career is kaput!"

After my shift, I went home to our apartment, which was an abandoned beehive. Arleta and I had just gotten married. I stood in the door for five minutes with tears in my eyes. I said, "Well, I thought I would do better than this. It's over!" Arleta said, "Just give it thirty days. If you don't like it after a month, you can always go back to your old job."

I was fortunate the program director, George Dunlevy, convinced the manager I had talent and they should give me a chance as a DJ. They put up with any errors I made in the beginning. In a month's time, I became more proficient working the equipment, more fluid in filling in with silly jokes. Once I knew what I was doing, everything clicked. Which brings me to another important point: Don't give up easily. I was ready to give up too quickly. Instead of giving up, I practiced the skill of running turntables, pacing my show better, and transforming into an on-air personality. Typically, it takes a while, especially if you are not skilled at it, but everyone learns differently. I was a fast learner, because within three months, I became the number one disc jockey in Omaha, beating out Todd Storz's station KOWH, which until then had dominated the morning airwaves. It turned out to be a lucky break for me.

After my experience at KOIL, I became number one in every city where I've worked and gained not only more confidence but also increasingly better opportunities for myself. I moved to KIMN in Denver to become its morning man, then WNOE in New Orleans, where I was a troubleshooter for Gordon McLendon and Don Keyes. I'd improve the station's ratings, then move up a step in salary.

I first came to California when I was sixteen, traveling with my neighbor Lee Harris. We told our folks we were going to Iowa, but instead headed over the Rockies to the West Coast in a car with very bad brakes. When I saw California, with the ocean and the palm trees, I said, "This is where I wanna be!" Many years later, while I was a DJ at WIL in St. Louis, Chuck Blore, one of the great legends of broadcasting, offered me a job at KEWB in San Francisco. At first I didn't accept the offer, but that night, a tornado hit St. Louis. The next day I headed west, where I was fortunate in topping Don Sherwood of KSFO in the ratings. Don had been unbeatable in that market for many years.

From San Francisco, in 1961, I went to work for KFWB, Top 40 heaven in Los Angeles, where we had a giant audience of five million people per day. We were called the KFWB "Good Guys," and practically every rock-and-roll station in America copied our music format and us. Our lineup of on-air personalities included Bill Ballance, Eliot Field, Joe Yocum, Gene Weed, B. Mitchell Reed, Ted Quillen, Ted Randall, Roger Christian (who wrote many of the Beach Boys songs), and me. Chuck Blore, the vice president of programming, had specific rules for us: limit the amount of chatting between records, and create an imperceptible overlap going from a commercial or jingle right into the music.

From KFWB, I jumped to KMPC, where I spun such classic sounds as Frank Sinatra and Ella Fitzgerald. I was top afternoon-drive radio personality for Gene Autry's Golden West Broadcasters for twenty consecutive years. With the ears of Hollywood's movers and shakers listening, that position led to cartoons, commercials, television, movies, and more voice work than I ever could have imagined.

I've been fortunate to win many honors in broadcasting—the Radio Hall of Fame, the National Association of Broadcasters Hall of Fame (inducted for both radio and television), and *Billboard* naming me the World's Top Radio Personality. On June 11, 2003, I was voted L.A.'s Top Radio Personality of All Time by my peers in broadcasting (every radio station in Los Angeles voted!). The honor was reported in Don Barrett's book *Los Angeles Radio People*. I don't think I would have achieved this success without having worked in radio with training wheels at first. Working in a small market has its advantages. While the wages can be small by comparison, the opportunities to grow creatively can be wonderful and beneficial to you in the long run. If you grow as you go and make it work, each avenue will only get better. Each time you move to another market, you will increase your salary and improve your standard of living. It will become a stepping-stone to more money, more success.

Step 3: Always Be a Student

Knowing the business inside and out is vital to your future success. Always be a student and never get complacent. I have always read every industry magazine I could find—*Radio & Records, Billboard, Variety, Hollywood Reporter, Cash Box, Record World, Inside Radio, The Gavin Report, Radio Ink,* and *Broadcasting* magazine. I did this to learn the names of the movers and shakers in the business—who was doing what, which disc jockeys were jumping to other stations, and who owned what stations. I got to know this guy at WFIL in Philadelphia and that guy at WITH in Baltimore, plus top 40 mavens like Paul Drew, Bill Drake, and Ron Jacobs. This proved very helpful when I went to radio or broadcasting conventions. I began to know the names of people at stations, and when I met them in person, I found out more about them and the business. Knowledge of your field and the ability to network are valuable assets.

When seeking employment, always know the call letters of the stations before dropping in on them. KMPC was kind enough to take out this gigantic billboard so I wouldn't forget.

It's important to stay connected with not only changes but also with those who make the major decisions that affect everyone. To that end, today, I continue to speak at most of the major broadcasting conventions.

Step 4: Know Station Call Letters When Seeking Employment

When seeking employment as a disc jockey, be sure you know the call letters of the stations before dropping in on them. I remember when Willie Nelson was first starting as a recording artist; he and Kenny Rivercomb, an executive with Liberty Records, made stops throughout the state of Georgia to promote Willie's new album. In doing so, they saw the letters W-I-G-S at the top of a building and walked right in. Kenny said, "Can we see your music director?"

The person on the other end said, "We don't have a music director." Then they said, "Can we see your program director?"

The person who worked there said, "Well, there's no program director."

Kenny said, "Well, we've got this new album featuring Willie Nelson. He's such a great singer, and we thought that you could play it for us."

The guy said, "Wait just a minute. Let me get the manager for you."

The manager walked over, and Kenny introduced himself and Willie again. "Hi, I'm Ken Rivercomb, and this is Willie Nelson."

"How do you do?" The manager and he shook hands.

Kenny said, "We'd like to give these albums to you so you can play them on the air."

The manager looked perplexed. "We don't play anything on the air."

Kenny said, "Well, you're a radio station. We saw your call letters: W-I-G-S."

The manager laughed. "Sir, we sell toupees. We're a wig store."

Step 5: Develop a Great On-Air Personality

What makes a great radio personality? Someone who's different, provocative, and clever. Today disc jockeys can be more cutting-edge than they were when I started. Radio personality Royce Johnson lost his job when a competitor recorded him using the sound effect of a toilet flushing on the air. The Federal Communications Commission wanted to take the station's license. Instead, Royce lost his job. That was in 1957. Radio's changed a lot since then! Howard Stern is cutting-edge radio, and being a shock jock is where it's at for many in the business.

Radio is a wonderful platform on which you can develop your personality, style, and humor and be distinctive doing it. It's a business that can provide great joy and great opportunities, and one of the only media in the world where you can use your imagination and be totally creative and spontaneous at the same time. There are numerous other qualities besides these that are important.

On radio, your voice is your personality. Having a pleasant voice that sounds casual and comfortable on the air or with a microphone is important. As a radio personality, you want to sound like you're having a regular conversation with a friend, except that your friend might happen to be fifty thousand listeners.

On radio the tone of your voice and the way you come across matter. For example, an afternoon rock-and-roll show will have a different tone than a late-night blues show. For jazz, the on-air personality's voice needs to be smooth and assuring to match the style of the show. When you're talking to your listeners, it's important to convey the right sound in your voice to fit the theme of your show.

Preparation is the key, and you can never be overprepared. Gordon McLendon and Don Keyes of the McLendon Corporation and Chuck Blore of Crowell-Collier Broadcasting taught me how to prepare for radio. Gordon taught me to do one hour of preparation off the air for every hour on the air. If you are on the air for three hours a day, then you should take three hours to prepare, whether you're writing down jokes, gathering ideas, or planning which songs to play.

Generally, I carefully plan my broadcast to make each show different. I write down the first line of every commercial and plan a lead-in, or what I'm going to say before the commercial. The same goes with introducing the cuts of music. Ahead of time, I prepare some lines that lead into a song, something like, "Y'know, I learned to be a swell dancer when I was a little kid. My tricycle had a loose seat! In a moment, I'll tell you how the cup of life turned out to be a dribble glass, but before I do, here's Frank Sinatra singing 'My Way.'" Then I'll cue the song. Other times I'll take a line from a commercial and use that in my show. For example, if the announcer in the commercial is talking about the Diner's Club card, he might say, "It's the best news yet." Before running that commercial, I'll cue up that line, "It's the best news yet." Then I'll say something silly like, "In a moment, I'm going to let the air out of my head" (Voice-over: "It's the best news yet!"), then cue up the real commercial.

Disc jockeys need to have a good sense of timing. It's as though you're a conductor orchestrating the whole show. It's important to have the imperceptible overlap of music and voice dovetail so it is like the tip of one touching the other as you segue your show, making your segues smooth and clean, not abrasive. First you may announce your show and then hit a jingle. The jingle ends, and a commercial immediately starts, followed by another commercial. You come back and maybe make a joke or provide information of some kind and then introduce a song. You're constantly orchestrating your show.

Step 6: Find a Good Boss and Stick with Him or Her

Aside from the qualities we've just described that make a great on-air personality, finding a boss who loves your work can lengthen your radio career. The average stay for a disc jockey is only one and a half years. Change for change's sake is not always good. "The grass is always greener" may work for some. You must trust your bosses until you get to know them and go from there.

Much of my phenomenal success on radio I owe to one man who was a champion to me (and so was his horse): the great cowboy star Gene Autry. I worked for Gene for twenty years at KMPC and Golden West Broadcasters. I enjoyed working there—each day was euphoric—and I enjoyed the atmosphere. Gene thought it was wonderful that I was involved in so many forms of entertainment, because he knew from his own experience that one form promotes the other.

Gene gave me one of his own white Stetson hats like those he wore in his many movies. Whenever he was in his office, down the hall from mine on the second floor of 5858 Sunset Boulevard next to Bronson Avenue (the name of this street inspired Charles Buchinsky to change his name to Charles Bronson!), we'd sit and talk baseball. He owned the California Angels—now Anaheim Angels—for many years. As a kid, he wanted to be a major leaguer himself. Instead, he ordered his first guitar out of a Sears Roebuck catalog and paid $8 for it, and as they say, the rest is history.

Gene was always good to me. He let me use Harry Truman's desk in my office. At one time, Truman had an office at Golden West Broadcasters. They put cork on the walls of my office, and I told manager Stan Spero, while they were installing it, I was allergic to that. He came in, sat down at my desk, and said, "How do you like your office?" Before I could

Having a boss who loves your work can lengthen your radio career, as I experienced with Gene Autry at KMPC. Gene is all smiles in this photo taken after Larry King told him that he had double-parked his horse.

answer, he started sneezing and sneezed for ten minutes. The next day, the cork came down, and walnut paneling went up. Stan was a great manager, and I cherish my twenty years with him.

I emceed many events where Gene was honored with tremendous awards. He would always say, "I certainly don't deserve this award, but I've got arthritis, and I don't deserve that either!"

I feel honored to have worked with Gene and to have known him. He was always a gentleman and a great friend to me.

Step 7: Give Your Openings Purpose

Success as a disc jockey takes the right blend of ingredients. The first one is opening your show with something clever or humorous, like a joke or a funny bit that sets the stage for things to come. I've always made my producer or engineer a character on my radio show, starting with my career as "Josh Dickey." Obviously, it helps to have a producer or engineer with a sense of humor. If not, paying them obscene sums of money works. Here are some sample openings to my daily radio show over the years to illustrate:

> "Hi, welcome to 'The Gary Owens Show.' I'm here with my engineer . . .

> " . . . Bud Stalker, who's been out stalking Buds at the brewery."

> " . . . Wayne DuBois, who's gnawing on his couch."

> " . . . Larry Reed, having some delicious alphabet soup like his mother used to spell."

> " . . . Clayton 'Bud' Wormsbecker, who's just been devoured by a group of wild turkeys."

> " . . . Jason Jeffries, who's just invented a new chicken soup, and he's just discovered no chicken will drink it."

> " . . . Birdie, who was seen yesterday walking through the car wash with her dinner dishes!"

> " . . . Jeff Gehringer, who reminds you it's best not to eat anything left out on the Ventura Freeway for more than five days!"

> " . . . 'sniling' Jack Foster, who has a transistor radio so small he only gets Garfunkle on it!"

> " . . . Bob Moudis, who is just having his dessert now. He thinks chocolate cake is the best because it doesn't show the dirt as easily."

> " . . . Mike Crozier, who likes his coffee very strong. He's the only guy I know who eats it with a spoon right out of the can."

Step 8: Have a Sense of Humor

Developing a good sense of humor that is inoffensive and will appeal to a cross-section of listeners is vitally important. Using appropriate humor and keeping it that way for the airwaves helps if you want people to laugh. When developing jokes, think of what people are talking about around the water cooler besides cursing their boss for not giving them a raise. Or you could be like me and possess an irreverent sense of humor.

Al Lohman, a great radio broadcaster, former partner, and friend, once gave me the highest compliment. He said, "Gary, you were doing *Airplane* twenty-five years before the movie." I suppose that's true, because I was always a little different from most on-air personalities. Many disc jockeys would do jokes; I would do improv—comedy bits, like comedy soap operas with sound effects and other voices. I could take a sound effect—I have about ten thousand sound effects and wild tracks that I use on my radio show at any point in time—and music and do something funny with them. Or I'd do a whole bit with a play on words or the kind of double entendre that was later seen in the *Airplane* and *Naked Gun* movies. People never knew what to expect, and because of that, they kept listening. Yet I can't take all the credit for my success. I had a wonderfully talented comedy troupe of regulars who would come on my radio shows to do funny bits of business with me.

Bob Arbogast, best known for the "Arbogast and Pete Show" featuring partner Pete Robinson on Chicago's WMAQ, was one of my many early comedy influences from radio. At KMPC, Arbo was one of my regulars. I would do all kinds of things involving funny word play with him. To wit:

> **G.O.:** It's Waltz Time.
> **Arbogast:** What time is it, Walt?
> **G.O.:** 3:15.
> **Arbogast:** Thanks, Walt!
> **G.O.:** You've been listening to Waltz Time!

I created many different characters and offbeat bits that I used on my show. They featured a cast of crazies, all program regulars, including comedian–movie star Albert Brooks; Ken Levine, now a successful television producer who produced "Cheers" and "Frazier"; John Rappaport, who later became a writer for "Laugh-In" and produced the Emmy

Having a good sense of humor is vitally important, too, as Lucille Ball reminded my wife, Arleta, and me.

Award–winning series "M*A*S*H"; and Tom Straw—who produced "Night Court," "The Bill Cosby Show," and "Whoopi Goldberg."

During the California Angels baseball season on KMPC (for years the Angels' flagship station), my son Chris was eight years old when he played Dwayne Fimmerton, a kid who was a baseball fan on my show. He knew everything about the team and the players, including Rogers Hornsby's batting average, and we would phone the Angels' second base-man Bobby Knopp live on air. I would say, "Call the Knopps." Chris would say, "OK," and then I would cue a police siren sound effect. "No, not the cops!—the Knopps!"

Utilizing your friendships with known stars, be they in rock, adult contemporary, country, adult standard, or pop, is another way to add humor to your show, especially if your friends reveal some hidden talent or something few people have known about them. Because of my friendship with Paul Stewart and Everett Sloan, who worked with Orson Welles on *Citizen Kane* and many Mercury Theater presentations, I revealed, for the first time anywhere, the real meaning of "Rosebud" in the classic movie. Another time, Ringo Starr of the Beatles beat a paradiddle on a fan's collarbone to the tune of "Lady Madonna"—all in good fun, of course.

When it comes to doing anything humorous, remember to keep your humor current and topical. You can always reuse jokes that worked in the past and simply update or change them to make them more applicable to current events. Everyday situations and common problems can be another great source of humor and will help your audience relate to you.

Don't ask me why, but one of the "rules" of comedy is that any word that has the letter *k* in it is funnier than one that doesn't. Take, for example, *ickle*, *mickle*, and *pickle* versus *mud*, *coat*, *blasphemy*. See? Everything is funnier with a *k*.

Jokes for all occasions still make listeners laugh. They don't always have to be topical or current to make people snicker. Knock-knock jokes still work. I did a whole series of bad knock-knock jokes. Here's one example:

"Knock-knock."

"Who's there?"

"The Invisible Man is outside."

"Tell him I can't see him."

In radio broadcasting, I've always used gags for the cross-promotion of the other personalities on the station or network, even as far back as my first DJ job. Cross-promotion is a major part of broadcasting for radio or TV, and an integral part of your success. Your cohorts plug you and your show, and you mention them daily and talk about what they have planned—an interview with Britney Spears or the mayor, or a theme show about Elvis.

By doing this, you serve several purposes. First, you come across like a team player. Second, it fosters goodwill from your colleagues, who won't mind as much if your show still gets better ratings than theirs. Finally, and most importantly, this technique can generate higher ratings and ad revenue, which is necessary if stations are to be profitable and successful. The more people listen or tune in, the better ratings will be, and ultimately, the station can charge more for commercial time from its advertisers.

Of course, when doing cross-promotion, it's best to do more than just mention another personality's name and the time that person is on the station. One of the best ways to cross-promote is to use humorous one-liners. Whatever you say should be memorable and entertaining. I would say things like this:

> *"Bill Ballance, my chum, will be here tomorrow on Channel 98 KFWB! I love the sign he has in his office: 'Do unto others like you were the others!'"*

> *"Rick Dees will be here tomorrow morning. He's hosting a TV game show called 'Life's Unfair,' where no one wins any prizes."*

> *"Daisy Torme likes to go to her grandmother's house on Thanksgiving—she owns a McDonald's!"*

> *"Wink Martindale will be wearing his Hawaiian shirt out at Foonman's Miniature Golf Course in Sherman Oaks, complete with obstacles—the main one being the price."*

> *"Brad Chambers will be here to read excerpts from the famous Lincoln-Mercury debate."*

> *"Be sure and hear Jim Duncan tomorrow midmorning on the Fab 570 KLAC. Jim pointed out yesterday that on that date in 1969, strange things happened in the world of rock and roll. The group Sha Na Na lost a 'Na.'"*

It is not necessary to use humor. You can talk about the host being an empathetic individual or a schmuck, depending on his or her personality, of course.

Step 9: Develop Zany Giveaways

Doing zany giveaways on the air is a tremendous way to keep listeners coming back for more. People love getting free stuff.

Today, many stations still do giveaways. Primarily, they are done to attract more listeners, including people who have never tuned in before. The promotion department of the radio station, which has a budget for this kind of thing, handles them. The same department dreams up most promotional ideas for the station. Others are suggested by DJs as a way to pump up ratings.

I hosted a lot of unusual giveaways in Los Angeles. One year I gave away fifty thousand copies of an autographed picture of the Harbor Freeway, which most of the time was backed up in traffic and the bane of everyone's existence, signed, "Yours Very Truly, Harbor Freeway" or "Love, Harbor Freeway."

I ran a Complete Failure Club while working at radio stations in St. Louis and San Francisco. Anybody who had ever been a failure in their life could get one of these cards. People would mail us a self-addressed, stamped envelope, and we'd send the card back to them.

Another time, I offered the Gary Owens Jigsaw Puzzle (two pieces). No matter how you put it together—it's like the world today—it doesn't quite fit. Those kinds of things weren't necessarily done frequently.

Zany giveaways are sure to heighten the public's perception. Thousands of people out of curiosity will send in for whatever you are offering. Just make sure the host's name and station call letters—WLS, WNEW, KISS-FM, or whatever—are on it, plus the dial position, AM or FM.

Step 10: Stage Silly Promotions and Promotional Events

One way to draw attention to your station and promote yourself at the same time is to stage events that will attract the press. If you are a student at a high school or college station, you can promote yourself with clever giveaways. You don't need a big budget—as long as you ask your listeners

Courtesy: Fred Wostbrock.

Staging silly public events can be a wonderful way to publicize yourself. Here I am leading the pack before the start of the World's Shortest Parade. Pictured behind me are (over my shoulder) Albert Brooks, a gargoyle, starlet Bob Arbogast (sucking his thumb), and a guy pretending to play the tuba.

to include a self-addressed, stamped envelope in their request for what you are giving away!

The McLendon radio chain was always big on promotions. At a Lion's Club auction, our program director, Don French, brought an actual lion, thinking this would be a great gimmick for public events. One day, while driving on the freeway, Don looked at the lane next to him and, surprised, saw his lion in the cage looking back at him. The trailer hitch had broken, and his feline friend was cruising down the highway on his own. The trailer careened off the road into a tree, not hurting Mr. Lion or any commuters. It was a great bit of good fortune. Don French, who loved to party, had seen pink elephants cavorting before, but never the king of beasts having one for the road.

Developing clever on-air promotions can improve your ratings. Here I am with the winner of the Phyllis Diller Look-Alike Contest at the Lavish Gary Owens Building at KMPC. The lovely winner is seen opening a box of high-fashion dirndls.

My all-time favorite act of buffoonery was at the Hollywood Bowl. In 1973 I produced the Gary Owens Minute at the Bowl to promote my new album, *Put Your Head on My Finger*, for MGM Records and produced by Mike Curb and Michael Viner. We purposely had twenty-five press people there and eighteen thousand empty seats. I rented the Hollywood Bowl and had a sign maker put up a sign that read, "Gary Owens at the Hollywood Bowl—Sold Out!"

The show was a nonstop cavalcade of crazy antics. Alan Katz wore a dog suit and barked the song "Trees." Ruth Buzzi sang, "You'll Never Walk Alone," and Donna Jean Young tap-danced to it. Sarah Kennedy played electric guitar with a scalp vibrator. Richard Dawson did rude birdcalls in a tuxedo. Pat McCormick, who had never dropped his pants at the Bowl, dropped them in my honor. Jack Riley walked in the water fountain near the stage until his hat floated. Bob Arbogast and Jack Margolis did their world-famous headstand where Jack would lie down flat on the floor and Arbo would stand on Margolis's head. A Glendale pharmacist recited two prescriptions in Latin while alternately playing the tuba. People just did ludicrous things. *Billboard* and *Hollywood Reporter* both called it "the greatest entertainment event of all time."

Another time I hosted the World's Shortest Parade. Albert Brooks, Bob Arbogast, and I held a parade at UCLA, and the press came out to cover it. As cameramen and news crews sprang into action, we all lined up. I announced the start of the parade. We all took one half step backward, and the parade was over!

I have also utilized many famous guests on my shows for promotional gimmicks, such as unusual contests. On several occasions, Lon Chaney Jr., best known as the Wolfman in classic Universal horror movies, would come on my show at KMPC. I would hold a special Halloween contest in which I asked listeners to tell us, in twenty-five words or less, why they would like Lon to bite them on the neck! I also did a Phyllis Diller Look-Alike Contest, from which I chose a woman who didn't look anything like Phyllis as the winner!

Fans loved these productions. Their joy is they are nonsensical. That's the beauty of them. They capture the imagination. Fans remember the show and create conversation, as my friend Matty Simmons did with *National Lampoon* magazine for years, always tongue in cheek.

Step 11: Keep Your Pride and Joy

Among many things I've learned during my years in the business is, at all times, to keep my pride and joy. One of my favorite comedians was Henny Youngman ("Take my wife, please!"). Henny and I were sitting and chatting in 1968 when we were doing "Rowan and Martin's Laugh-In." He said, "Owens, have I shown you my pride and joy?"

I presumed he was referring to his grandchildren. "No, you haven't, Henny."

He reached into his wallet and took out a small business card. On it was a picture of two detergents—a bottle of "Pride" and a container of "Joy."

Step 12: When All Else Fails, Nurny Yourself

Some years ago, the talented entertainer Paul Reid and I wrote a piece of music called "The Nurny Song." The lyrics were simple: "Nurny nurny nurny—Nurny nurny nurny, nurny nurny nurn—F'nork!" (F'nork was a noise made when an animated cartoon character I played, Roger Ramjet, would hit an evildoer in the mouth.)

Almost every guest we had in our KMPC studios in Hollywood would record "The Nurny Song" on tape. Over five hundred stars have done for it me, including such talents as Frank Sinatra, Dean Martin, Neil Diamond, and Dionne Warwick. So, "nurny" yourself today. You'll be glad you did.

Always Impress Others

It pays to impress others, since your first impression may be your last. When Paul Newman was getting set to star in the movie WUSA, Paramount Pictures had to do research on what radio personalities did during the broadcast of an actual show. So they asked me if they could watch me do my show.

At 3:05 that afternoon, Paul and his entourage showed up at the KMPC studios. Now, this was not a typical day because at 6:00 P.M., I had to scoot down the street and co-emcee the Grammy Awards at the Hollywood Palladium with Bill Cosby.

Because I had no time to change, I was already wearing a tuxedo and had my makeup on. I was doing a show with the Silly Jingle Singers up loud with them purposely mispronouncing my name "Gary Onems," with Paul looking puzzled the whole time.

Next I called for a sound effect of a guy tap-dancing. It was my Clinton S. Feemish voice, and he was tap-dancing to the weather forecast. A sound of a man hiccuping and falling down the stairs followed. Then I went to several prerecorded commercials. This continued for the next couple of hours, and Paul Newman and his entourage had taken many notes. Finally, I asked, "Any questions?"

The legendary movie star looked at me with his baby blue eyes and said, "Do you always wear a tuxedo and makeup for radio?"

I said, "Of course!"

He smiled and sauntered out of the studio as the women at KMPC all swooned.

Always Know Your Guests' Names

You often can enliven your broadcasts by having wonderfully witty and well-known guests on your show. I've had hundreds of celebrities, actors, actresses, sports figures, and the men who press my suits on my radio shows over the years. If you want to be successful, knowing the names of your guests ahead of time helps. Do your guests the courtesy of researching information about them, so you can conduct an informed interview!

I found this to be true when I did my first network radio broadcast with Duke Ellington for the Mutual Broadcasting System at the ripe age of seventeen. My buddy had written the script that morning, and I really hadn't had time to look it over until we were ready to broadcast. Instead of saying, "The Duke is on the air," in the introduction, he wrote, "Duck." When I glanced at the script, I thought, "Well, there must be some reason for this," and I said it that way. "The Duck is on the air." Duck, er, Duke Ellington, had earphones on and looked up at me like, "What?" Somehow I survived the faux pas.

Above All Else, Always Answer Your Fan Mail

In doing both local and national radio shows for over four decades, I've received bushels of fan mail featuring myriad questions and comments about my program. It's important to connect with your fans, since they are the whole reason you have a successful career in radio. I've made it a practice to respond personally to as many fans as possible. I'm still amazed by the outpouring of love, admiration, and kudos my fans have bestowed upon me over the years. Here's one example:

Dear Gary,

All I can say is that to me you seem cold—without true emotion—planning, calculating all the time—constantly extracting the maximum advantage from the slightest opportunity that arises. It appears you subject all emotions and feelings to the demands of pragmatic reason.

Your pal,

Mother

Oops! Wrong letter. Well, let me see if I can come up with a better example. On second thought, maybe not. This is probably a good time to move on to the next chapter, on becoming a famous news announcer, before my face turns the color of a giant turnip.

5

Making News Broadcasting Your Business

THE GLOBAL RISE of satellite radio and television and the phenomenal growth of cable television have had a profound effect on news broadcasts. Perhaps the most noticeable change is the growing demand for newscasters, weather forecasters, and sports reporters on both radio and television. Radio is an instant and reliable news source that delivers up-to-the-minute news locally, nationally, and around the world; more people still derive their first news of the day from radio than any other medium. With improved satellite uplink capability and more mobility than before, television news is equally competitive as a source for cutting-edge news.

Being a news announcer, weather forecaster, or sports reporter can be an exciting profession. You're in the middle of what's happening. What you do in your job can make a difference in the world. It's also satisfying to know you're communicating information that is vital to people's lives. Possessing broadcast-quality voices, many of today's top newscasters, weather forecasters, and sports announcers have made their livelihood in this profession while working in commercials, public speaking, narration, and other fields using their voice.

As a young boy, I dreamed of becoming a famous newscaster and practiced reading stories from the daily newspaper into a recorder at the kitchen table. I would compare my work to that of famous newscasters of the day, like Walter Winchell, Lowell Thomas, and Edward R. Murrow. Listening to these great announcers, I developed my vocal style.

I landed my first radio job while still in high school, working summer relief as a newscaster at a small radio station. While I was in college the next year, the guy who was the regular newscaster at the station drove to California and loved it so much that he didn't return. So they made me the news director, my first big break.

As a newscaster, I learned a great deal about news announcing and reporting and the things that are important when applying for a job in the business—like giving potential employers only your name, rank, and the cereal you eat in the morning. If I may wax serious for a moment, the good news is that while the news business is vastly different today, the qualities and responsibilities of a newscaster remain much the same.

Qualities of a Successful News Personality

The most important responsibility of a news personality—by "news personality," I mean news anchors, news reporters, and sports reporters—is to inform the public. And what makes a great newscaster? According to many industry professionals I spoke to, these are the six most appealing qualities—especially to news directors:

Enthusiasm

One primary quality all great newscasters have in common is their tremendous enthusiasm on and for the job. It's important never to waver in your enthusiasm.

Aggressiveness

The most successful newscasters are those who are aggressive when it comes to reporting the news. (Remember, as a wise philosopher once said,

"He who hesitates is not only lost, but miles from the exit.") News directors don't like news people who are passive.

Energy

Being energetic and possessing a high amount of energy all the time is the third quality required. Working in this profession is highly demanding and draining at times. So to be a famous newscaster, you must always be "up" for the job.

Inquisitiveness

For a newscaster, it helps to have an inquisitive mind — to be well read and current on all issues. By this, I don't mean reading the Sunday comics section of the newspaper to see if Dennis menaced anyone today or if Drabble dribbled. The most successful newscasters on radio and television are knowledgeable about myriad subjects.

   The great Albert Einstein once said, "Knowledge is power." (He also was once quoted as saying, "Imagination is *more* important than knowledge." Even Albert was entitled to have an off day.) What Albert meant, I think, is having an inquisitive and creative mind is important.

   I've always had thousands of books in my home. I spend half of my time in bookstores or in libraries. I have a quest for knowledge. There are certain fun things that the only way to find out about them is by reading. Television can't teach all of that, but reading will. So read with the best of them. Be well-read in many different subjects of interest, and, who knows, you may soon become the Albert Einstein of newscasters in a town near you.

Versatility

Being versatile is the fifth most important quality as a newscaster, especially in small markets, where you may wear more than one hat — or a chicken suit.

   Early in my career, I worked in Denver in radio and television as a newscaster and DJ for KIMN in the morning. I then hosted a thirty-minute kids' show in the afternoon on a local television station, and thirty minutes later announced the news on the same TV station. For the kiddie show, I would dress in a clown suit, a duck outfit, or whatever I found in the prop department that day.

One time, I wore a puffed up chicken suit with nothing underneath but a T-shirt and shorts because the outfit was so hot. A friend stopped by to see me, and we stood in the hall talking for twenty-five minutes, and I lost track of time. The stage manager rushed up to me. "Gary, you've got three minutes until you get on camera to do the newscast."

Well, there was no way of getting out of the chicken suit in time. So I went on the air wearing this silly chicken outfit with the orange beak over my head. I was so worried about losing my job, I should have just done some jokes and said the regular newscaster was dead today or whatever came to mind, but I didn't. I read the four and a half minutes of news in a chicken outfit. I can just imagine what people watching were thinking. Many years later, Allan Burns and Jim Brooks used this incident as a sketch on "The Mary Tyler Moore Show"—with Ted Knight.

Strong News Sense

News directors want news announcers who have a strong instinct for news, someone who likes to eat, drink, and sleep news, and who can get the story *right* and isn't afraid to ask tough questions.

Five Common Traits of a Newscaster

Besides these inherent qualities, you must possess five common traits to be a successful newscaster: writing skills, news-gathering skills, people skills, announcing abilities, and an appealing on-air personality.

Good Writing Skills

Good writing and communication skills are required if you want to be a great newscaster. Good newscasters can't merely report the story well; in addition, they must be able to write well. That includes summing up the

Courtesy: Fred Wostbrock.

Being versatile is an important quality in a newscaster, especially in small markets, where you may wear more than one hat . . . or a Superman suit. With me (left to right) are John Rappaport, producer of "M*A*S*H," and Joe Landis of CBS Television.

story correctly, getting all the facts straight, and occasionally adding important-sounding words to your copy—even those you don't understand, like *cacophony*—to impress your viewers.

Of course, bad writing isn't the only problem you have to avoid as a famous newscaster. The biggest mistake most newscasters make is in overstating a point. Avoid this at all cost. These bloopers are examples of good reporting gone amok:

- "There's an overturned tractor-trailer heading north on Route 93." —Report in a radio station's morning traffic update

- "The bodies could not be identified because they were found facedown."—A reporter, reporting the discovery of two bodies under a bridge in rural Missouri

- "Doctors say the longer the babies live, the better chance they'll have at surviving."—From a local newscast

- "Today Lesbian forces invaded . . . no, sorry, that should be Lesbianese." — From a news report in the United Kingdom on a Lebanese conflict

Good News-Gathering Skills

Your ability to gather the news — and gather it correctly — is equally important. When you are assembling information for your story, accuracy is the key. So is knowing how to pronounce what you are reporting.

When I was a newscaster at KORN, I had never seen the word *Tehachapi* before. I'm from the Midwest, where Tehachapi, California, is not a commonly used city name. Well, a story came across the Associated Press wire one morning that a strong earthquake had struck this small desert town, and hundreds of people were shaken out of their beds. I didn't have a chance to read the story in advance, which, of course, you should always do.

I went on the air and announced, "It's one o'clock and time for KORN news. . . . Hundreds of residents in the small California community of . . . " I saw the word *Tehachapi*, and I didn't know what to say, so I didn't say anything. I just paused for a moment.

Reading past the name, I continued, ". . . where . . . residents scurried back and forth, dishware rattled, and windows plattered. Meanwhile, the mayor of . . . " I saw the word again, and I still wasn't sure what to say. So I just paused. Every time I saw the word *Tehachapi*, I pretended that we had gone off the air.

The station manager rushed in after I finished the news broadcast and said, "What's going on here? Is something wrong?"

I said, "Gee, I don't know. I guess we went off the air a couple of times."

After the broadcast, I looked up *Tehachapi* and made sure I knew how to pronounce it!

Good People Skills

Newscasters also need to possess good people skills for interviewing a range of people and personality types, both famous and little-known people. Having a gift of gab will help you persuade people to bare their soul and tell you everything they know. Even so, to be an effective newscaster, follow these two golden rules told to me by a former newscaster:

1. **Watch your p's and q's.** When interviewing people, you should follow these simple rules of etiquette: Be polite, be fair, be balanced, and don't ask the obvious—even when obviously you shouldn't be so obvious because even the guy you're interviewing knows you're being obvious by your obvious line of questioning, obviously. Here are some common mistakes made by news reporters who didn't follow this simple golden rule:

- "Am I cold? Why do you think I'm sitting here under these two small Africans [meaning afghans]?"—Elderly lady, incredulously, during a televised interview at her home
- "How awful! Do you still have an artificial leg?"—Asked by radio host after a listener said, "My most embarrassing moment was when my artificial leg fell off at the altar on my wedding day"
- "So did you see which train crashed into which train first?"—A talk radio interviewer, questioning a fifteen-year-old eyewitness to a head-on train collision (The answer he gave was, "No, they both ran into each other at the same time.")

2. **Don't be shocked by what others say.** The second golden rule is not to be alarmed by what people tell you. As a news reporter, you will experience some gruesome and unflattering things—nothing perhaps that will compare to the sight of your Cousin Earle drinking with a straw through his nose. Even so, this is where it's important to stay on task and keep your eye on the story at all times. You have a job to do.

I found this rule important when I was a news director. At age seventeen, I was assigned to do a live broadcast on the Mutual Broadcasting System with former president Harry Truman and Senator Hubert Humphrey. Sitting next to Mr. Truman, I was visibly nervous, and he picked up on it right away. He turned to me and said, "What's the matter, young man?"

I said, "Well, I'm a little nervous. I've never introduced a president before."

Newscasters need good reporting skills and a way with words. Famed newspaper scribe Walter Winchell told me this plus the first rule of reporting: to ditch the Jimmy Olson getup I was wearing. (Also, I had a frog under my hat!)

"You know, don't let that worry you," he said. "Whenever I speak or do any broadcast at all, I'm always scared shitless until I get on. Then I'm OK."

To this day, I've never forgotten this golden rule . . . or President Truman "scared shitless."

Good Announcing Abilities

A great newscaster has to be a good public speaker and not be afraid in front of the camera. Your general presentation (appearance, business manner, personality, and whether your toupee is on straight) counts greatly, and so does your ability to communicate with your audience. Part of that is being able to read well. Certainly, you can achieve this by enunciating your words carefully; speaking naturally; giving appropriate emphasis to the words, phrases, sentences, and paragraphs; and maintaining an upward and downward inflection in your voice as you are reading.

Here's a popular phrase you can try at home, in the shower, while dressing for work, or while downing a Danish in the morning. Repeat the following, raising and lowering the inflection of your voice, to create the perfect broadcast quality: "The clanking and banging of the refrigerator is absent in Frigidator."

Your inflection is a little off. So maybe try again: "The clanking and banging of the refrigerator is absent in Frigidator."

Definitely better.

Now try this one: "I am popular at parties even though part of the time I am too pooped to pop the party poppers." One more time, without popping all those *p*s. Our sound engineer just went deaf in his left ear.

I know these sentences are ridiculous, and they're meant to be. But even great newscasters start this way, and if you can read these silly idioms, well, then you're definitely ready to be a newscaster.

Good On-Air Personality

Newscasters must also be great performers on the air if they want to be successful. Your first responsibility is to report the news, weather, or sports, but viewers also want to come away feeling entertained. At some stations, they let people at home know you're the "fun" news people. A simple pat on the back or playful fist to the chin will work. So will complimenting your co-anchor on that nice new snood she's wearing!

Developing an on-air repartee with your co-anchor, weather forecaster, and sports announcer is also important. Maybe jump into on-air conversation and friendly banter with such snappy lines as "You sound like someone's standing on your lip." It's this kind of smart repartee that is bound to make you a rising star at some stations in broadcasting today.

Top Ten Ways to Become a Famous Newscaster

Paul Moyer, the talented longtime co-anchor of the award-winning weekday editions of Los Angeles's "KNBC Channel 4 News," offers up this Top

Courtesy: Fred Wostbrock.

Your announcing abilities matter greatly, too. When reading the news, keep all eyes on the copy—especially during a California earthquake, when this photo was taken.

Ten list. Paul, who has great experience in TV news broadcasting and is a winner of six Golden Mike awards and eight Emmy Awards for news, is one of the all-around good guys in the news business. He came up with the following list, which applies to anyone wanting to break into the business:

10. **Learn to devour newspapers at an early age.**

9. **Go to college.** Take political science, history, and all the writing classes you can get your hands on. Practice in front of a microphone or a mirror. Go to every radio and TV station in town, and beg for part-time work. Experience, experience, experience.

8. **Be willing to go anywhere at any time for that first full-time job.** And he means anywhere. For Paul, it was Sioux City, Iowa. Like me, he learned his trade when no one was watching. It was easier that way, and when the big market called, he was ready.

7. **Viewers can spot a phony faster than management can say, "We're not renewing your contract."** Don't try to be something or somebody you're not. Your style and personality will come to the surface if you let them, and that's what viewers want.

6. **Don't just read words and sentences.** Communicate ideas, attitude, emotion, and meaning. Tell stories! Do your homework. Know the stories you are telling. Care about them. If you don't, the viewers won't care about you.

5. **Never put yourself above your audience.** Don't talk down to them. Don't talk at them. Talk *to* them. Be honest about yourself, your work, and your mistakes. The viewers are comfortable with and respond to honesty. Trust and believability are your two most important tools. You can't buy them, and you can't peddle them. You earn them over time with consistency.

4. **Learn from criticism well meant, but never, ever let anyone try to mold you into a mirror of "everybody else."** Cookie-cutter anchors don't become franchise players.

3. **Don't watch yourself on tape too often.** Those who study themselves constantly can become too studied, too mechanical, too predictable, and too stiff on the air. It becomes more a performance and less a spon-

taneous telling of stories. Should you review your newscasts periodically for an occasional spot check for bad habits? Sure. Any more—don't do it.

2. Don't kiss butt, and don't trust those who do. Unless, of course, they think you're the greatest, and they are in upper management and can turn your career on a dime. Then, by all means . . .

1. Never speak ill of other anchors. Go in, do your work, and mind your own business. If you don't, you just might find out what they're saying about you.

Thanks, Paul! You're great.

Qualities of a Successful Weather Forecaster

Weather forecasters do more than interpret global, regional, and local weather patterns to make short- and long-range weather forecasts and point at blue screens with nothing on them. Because the weather images are projected onto a large TV monitor offstage, it takes tremendous eye-hand coordination to be a weather forecaster—and a very long neck. The four most important qualities required to be a weather forecaster are tolerance of difficulties, a sense of humor, flexibility, and love of excitement.

Ability to Rise to the Challenge

It pays to be thick-skinned if you want to work as a weather forecaster. You will be the intense subject of criticism most of the time. People think that because you're a weather forecaster, you really *are* Mother Nature—an insult to Mother Natures everywhere—and have complete control over the natural world, including whether it rains, snows, or is sunny every day.

Like Rodney Dangerfield, weather forecasters don't often get the respect they deserve, as Meclovio Perez, a local weatherman for Channel 2 News in Los Angeles, once found out. While he was doing a ski report, a bunch of male skiers, standing behind him, unbeknownst to him, decided to drop their trousers simultaneously and mooned him, all on live television. There was nothing Meclovio or the station could do, except make light of the situation and be sure that any future moon shots were of astronauts.

Tolerance for Some Egg on Your Face

With so much information to report and details to study every day, it's tough being a weather forecaster. Sometimes even the most meticulous forecasts can go awry, and you're apt to wind up with egg on your face — better scrambled than fried!

A Degree of Flexibility

If you want to be a weather forecaster, flexibility must be your middle name. If you have any other middle name, then you may want to choose another profession. Much like a news announcer, a weather forecaster is in a demanding profession. One minute it is sunny, the next cloudy, then storming or freezing cold. Having an extra pair of galoshes around at all times helps, even if you live in the desert. You never know when a monsoon might hit, and you'll be up to your kneecaps in cactus needles.

Ability and Desire to Take On a Career That Is Never "Dull"

As you can tell, being a weather forecaster is an ever-changing, exciting career choice. If you like excitement, if you like moving around a lot (and leaving no forwarding address), and if you like the weather, then you've passed the first hurdle to becoming a weather forecaster, and you've chosen the right profession.

Willard Scott's Nine Rules for Making a Great Weather Forecaster

Of course, to become a great weather forecaster, it helps to know one. I enlisted my dear friend, bestselling author and famous NBC weatherman Willard Scott, to give me his Top Nine list of what every person needs to know to become a famous weatherman like him. Here's what Willard said:

1. It helps to know something about weather.
2. Be fat and funny. Remember, you are a sidekick to the anchors, who are always gorgeous and thin.
3. Find out how to determine the dew point.
4. Discover and use the relative humidity. (That's basically the sweat you work up drinking with your cousin.)
5. Keep working on the dew point.
6. Remember, 86 degrees with no wind is perfect to be outdoors totally naked.
7. Keep working on the dew point.
8. *Always* remember you are the *real reason* people tune in to watch the news.
9. What the heck is dew point?

Thank you, Willard, for those wise and wonderful remarks. I'm certain that future weather forecasters everywhere thank you, too, and are reading up on dew point as we speak.

Common Mistakes to Avoid

A common mistake most weather forecasters make is using old data. Reading yesterday's newspaper isn't going to help you today. When studying, analyzing, or forecasting the weather, it is important to look at the date and time stamp on the image. Forecasting with new data will optimize your accuracy.

Of course, as a weather forecaster, sometimes you can give too little or too much information. It's important to find a happy medium that works for you so you won't be embarrassed when your weather forecast is off—like when forty inches of snow is suddenly dumped on the city, and you predicted a glorious, sunny 70-degree day. Here are examples of the two extremes you should avoid when doing your forecasts:

TOO GENERAL

Today the sun will rise. Expect some clouds with mostly cloudy conditions, some sun, returning to mostly cloudy conditions, then showers and thunderstorms and mostly cloudy conditions, cloudy most of the day, if not for returning sunshine and some clouds, but cloudy most of the time until sunset. The highs will be in the seventies, maybe the eighties or nineties, depending on how sunny or cloudy it is. The lows tonight will range from 40 to 60 degrees, with no chance of sun but certainly cloudy.

Even though it sounds like there's a good chance it will be cloudy, this example is too general of a forecast. The public will have a difficult time preparing their day for this type of forecast.

TOO SPECIFIC

Pack your galoshes, everybody. Expect increasing clouds with a 100 percent chance for afternoon thunderstorms. The rain will begin at 2:00 P.M., subside at 2:15 P.M., resume at 2:27 P.M., subside briefly, then return around 3:15 P.M., subside again (you know, stop for a while), then resume again at 4:00 P.M., subside (ridiculous, isn't it?) for a while, pour like the dickens at 4:20 P.M., and subside (this is it, folks) into the night before all hell breaks loose and it pours so much rain that maybe you'd better pack your boots!

Sometimes being too specific is not a good idea. Weather forecasters love nothing better than to have people shower them with kudos and adoration when their forecasts are 100 percent accurate. Exact or not, there are only so many isobars or dew point depressions viewers really care about—and so many galoshes. The goal is not to put your viewers to sleep. Just give us the weather!

There you have it. Everything you want to know about becoming a famous newscaster or weather forecaster. Sound like fun professions, don't they? But if you're still uncertain about what you want to do using your voice and if fast action is your game, there's always a career as a famous play-by-play sports announcer. Which, by the way, if you turn to the next page, you can learn all about.

6

The Fast-Paced World of
Sports Announcing

IF YOU LOVE action and excitement, thrills and spills, close calls and fist-fights—and that's only what happens in the parking lot before the game—then being a sportscaster is for you. It's a marvelous profession for many reasons: You get to see the games for free. You have nobody to block your view. You get paid for calling the sport you love. Plus you can eat as many hot dogs with all the mustard, pickles, relish, onions, and sauerkraut your stomach—and your producer in the booth—can stand.

Unlike people in other announcing or voice-over jobs, sportscasters work a range of different shifts, including day and night games and on weekends. Be prepared to work long hours at the beginning of your career. It's unlikely you will start off as the Monday-night sportscaster on a major network. Not even Al Michaels or Howard Cosell started at the top. You probably will have to begin at a small television station announcing high school games and, with a little luck, work your way up. One of the best ways to break into the business is to volunteer at a radio or television station to gain experience as an intern.

Television or radio sportscasting doesn't require a great amount of physical strength, but it requires good concentration, a great memory, a strong voice, lots of stamina, and a strong stomach for all those grilled Polishes. The most successful individuals in the business are those who are personable and have a way with words.

Job openings depend on what your qualifications are, where you live, what you know, and what you are willing to accept as starting pay. Many young sportscasters will work for little or nothing in order to get experience. Without experience, you won't go very far. Those with experience can command large salaries, and a few sportscasters are making literally millions. Small cities and towns are a great place to hone your skills.

Opportunities have never been better. Every day, new national and regional sports networks are being launched, and many "fringe" sports— and some that never made it past the drawing board, like underwater Nerf bowling—that previously were never covered are now being broadcast, creating jobs for up-and-coming beginners. Tremendous growth also continues in radio with all-sports or sports-talk radio stations, even in small markets.

Sportscasters and Color Analysts

There are two types of sports announcers: the sportscaster, who announces the game and adds commentary, and the color analyst (or color commentator), who fills in during lulls in the action and stoppages of play with unique insights to the game, often mixing information with humor.

Except for baseball, during intermission announcers discuss the game in general and recap events and talk about the statistics and relevant facts. After the game, depending on the sport, either the sportscaster or color analyst will rush down to the field or floor or locker room to interview the player who scored the winning touchdown, got the key hit in the game, or wrestled the umpire.

To be a great sportscaster or color analyst, you should first love sports and have a broad background of knowledge you can bring to the game.

Watching games, reading books, and researching and studying the area you want to cover (and not just playing your favorite Nintendo game) will help you learn.

Lots of preparation goes into calling a game. Most professionals arrive at the game early. They spend time memorizing the opposing team's players and numbers, their game statistics, and noteworthy performances; prepare notes for the broadcast; and get their food order in early. They find out who's injured, whether it's someone's birthday, and whether the coach was caught fraternizing with the team's mascot so they can mention it later on the air.

Being ready for the task often includes preparing for a pregame show, interviewing players and coaches from the home team about how they think the game will turn out, interviewing opposing players, and presenting relevant statistics to inform and entertain fans listening or watching at home.

As a play-by-play announcer, your day is long and involved. Your workday begins long before the first pitch, the first puck, or the first pass is thrown. Many hours of preparation occur both before and after the game. For a 7:30 night game in baseball, for example, most sportscasters arrive four hours before game time to get ready. At 3:25, the announcers usually pull their cars into the parking lot. At 3:30, they enter the ballpark and grab a cup of coffee in the clubhouse and meet with the team's manager to chat about the upcoming game and players. At 3:45, the announcers go up to the broadcast booth, surveying the field for a moment before getting down to business. At 3:50, they usually sit down and start preparing their notes for the broadcast. At 4:45, they test the microphone in the radio broadcast booth. At 5:00, they meet up with their broadcasting partner and share notes and other material they've gathered. They chat, reminisce, and grab another cup of coffee. At 5:15, they grab a bite to eat in the cafeteria or eat the food that is delivered to the broadcast booth. At 5:30, having enjoyed a quick dinner, they do last-minute preparations for the game. At 6:00, they enter the booth and get ready for the night's broadcast, reviewing lineups and relevant facts provided by the team's media relations director. At 7:30, the event begins, and the sports announcer and color analyst stand in front of the camera and introduce

Lots of preparation goes into sports announcing. This includes knowing who the players are and keeping your objectivity at all times. Here I am with Yankees baseball legend Mickey Mantle, who was playing in a game at USC's Dedeaux Field, along with Lyle and Kyle Fendishman, the conjoined twins who hit back-to-back home runs.

themselves to the viewing or listening audience. At 7:35, the first pitch is thrown, and the sportscasting and the comments begin.

The Golden Rules of Sportscasting

While sports broadcasting and play-by-play announcing need to be both informative and entertaining, doing sports announcing requires a delicate balance between skillfully describing what the viewer sees on television or doesn't see on radio and providing your audience with information that the camera doesn't always pick up. For the report to be successful, developing a good working relationship is very important. So is developing a good rhythm and flow to your work as a team. To become the best in the business, whether you are the play-by-play announcer or the color analyst, follow these simple golden rules:

Play-by-Play Announcer
1. Communicate key happenings in a game, and provide your insight into what's going on.
2. Provide more information than necessary for your radio listeners so they can visualize what's happening (except in the event of a player's bad case of jock itch).
3. During television broadcasts, comment on the game and interpret events not picked up by the camera during a game.
4. Talk intelligently during the broadcast.
5. Never make events in the game more important than they are.
6. Avoid using too many sports clichés.
7. Don't overdo discussing statistics and bore your audience.
8. When announcing television play-by-play, be careful of doing too much or too little commentary.
9. Report only what you know is true; never guess about information.
10. Repeat the score frequently throughout the game. (Unless, of course, your team is losing 40–0; then break more frequently for commercials.)
11. When possible, report scores of other games, especially those of key opponents.
12. Be honest. Don't keep telling the audience how great the game is when it really isn't.
13. Don't guess in identifying a player. Cover the action, and give the name of the player when you're sure of it.
14. Provide relevant statistics, records, and other information that keeps fans informed.
15. Use only information that you need.

Color Analyst

1. Be original. Don't repeat what the play-by-play announcer says.
2. Don't comment on every play or everything. If you have nothing to say, keep quiet.
3. Strive to be accurate with your commentary. When you're wrong, admit it.
4. Do your homework and study both teams.
5. Be objective in your reporting without overly dramatizing the game.
6. If the play-by-play announcer makes a mistake, never correct him or her on the air.
7. State differing points of view, and remain friendly in your conversation.
8. Ask intelligent questions that draw the play-by-play announcer into your coverage of the game.
9. Never interrupt the play-by-play when the game is in progress. Wait until the play ends before speaking.
10. Follow the same rules as the play-by-play announcer so you're both on the same page of the playbook.

Play-by-Play Wisdom to Live By

One of the greatest names in sports broadcasting is Hall of Famer Vin Scully, the voice of the Los Angeles Dodgers. A few years back, Vin and I talked on my national radio show about what ingredients are necessary to become a successful sportscaster. Here's a summary of his comments:

■ Don't speak with your heart. Even though you think the world of your home team, if they're rotten, say so. See things with your eyes and your head.

■ Be thorough. Know the rules of the game. If you have to, explain the rules in a simple way, but don't talk down to your audience.

- Don't come on too strong in your play-by-play. When a great play does occur, you won't have already used up a year's supply of superlatives.

- You should make your dialogue conversational. It should sound like you're with a pal, discussing every play.

- Learn to report in a sequential manner: There's the pitch. Then the batter swings. Then, as the sportscaster, you follow the batted ball first. You see where it lands, and then you check the base runners.

- Always tell it like it is. Don't second-guess the players. If somebody goofs and boots the ball, don't try to make excuses for him.

- Try to use statistics sparingly, and utilize anecdotes about the players.

Approaches to Calling the Game

When it comes to sportscasting, radio and television differ in their approaches. A complete word picture is necessary for sports in radio broadcasting. On the flip side, television requires the announcer to supply captions for the picture being telecast.

The TV monitor is a very important tool (so is a Black & Decker head polisher for players who have shaved their noggin). The sportscaster uses the monitor to see the same picture that is transmitted to the viewer's screen and will confine his or her remarks to what is shown to the viewer at home. The play-by-play commentary has to be synchronized to the pictures the sportscaster sees on the monitor.

On radio, this is less important. Sometimes announcers are busy adjusting their headsets and adding mustard to their hot dog and get a few seconds behind. But the listener sitting at home can't tell.

Another thing that differs when calling sports on television is that the announcer always has to keep an eye on the ball and cannot presume the TV cameras will be showing the game all the time. In other words, don't be gawking at the cheerleaders when the quarterback is passing.

Because sports don't deal with politics, a sportscaster has great freedom to say what he or she wants. As long as sportscasters can respect the public, morality, and reason, there should be no problem with censorship.

The sportscaster should, at all times, strive for accuracy, although one of the greatest sportscasters of all time, Bill Stern, who worked at NBC, used his imagination if he missed seeing a play. Bill's associates would say that if he didn't notice who had the ball on a touchdown play, he would fabricate what happened: "Zordman, at quarterback on the four-yard line, laterals the ball to Yutz, who scores for Columbia." According to legend, if Bill didn't see the play, he would manufacture a lateral, and because it was radio and not TV, who knew? Someone once asked why the network didn't let Bill do the play-by-play at the Kentucky Derby, and the reply was, "Because you can't lateral a horse!"

If you're reporting baseball, your description should center on the batters and baserunning, offensive activity, or the teams' pitching and defensive ability. Check the coaching signs, the stance of the batter, his average, his eccentricities, his superstitions (he wears Jello under his cap), his RBIs, his season average. You can ad-lib about his personal weaknesses—maybe he's in the middle of a hitting streak or has set a record for kicking the water cooler for striking out eighty-nine straight times. This adds color to the broadcast for your listeners or viewers at home.

It's important for a sportscaster to bring fans into the game and to keep them interested throughout the entire broadcast. Nothing will do that better than talking about what has happened on the field, in the clubhouse, or on the court and getting some real juicy material to add to your broadcast.

Wilt Chamberlain told me a story about when he was at the University of Kansas. In those days, his coach would bench him in order to keep the score competitive. One night against Missouri, the coach benched him, with the score something like 65–45 in favor of Kansas. Missouri closed the gap to about eight points. A Missouri fan said to her boyfriend, "We're doing OK." The guy said, "Yeah, but I hope we don't do any better, or they'll put Chamberlain in again."

Another of my acquaintances in the big and tall department is the legendary Kareem Abdul Jabbar, well over seven feet, three inches tall. I played in the Celebrity Baseball game with Kareem for years at Dodger

Stadium. After UCLA and before his days with the Los Angeles Lakers, Kareem was a great star for the Milwaukee Bucks. His coach Larry Costello said, "You could cut him in two, and he'd make a pair of All-American guards."

Basketball coaches have their share of funny moments, too. The Cleveland Cavaliers, under coach Bill Fitch, were flogged by the Los Angeles Lakers one night. Fitch announced that high scorer Johnny Johnson was going to be coming out of the army as a "hardship case." A sports reporter asked Fitch, "What kind of hardship?" Bill said, "Us."

The legendary football coach John McKay and I used to be on the Sun Giant Almonds television and radio spots for years. John, the great University of Southern California football coach and later NFL coach of the Tampa Bay Buccaneers, was playing golf with one of his assistant coaches. He was just about to hit a wood shot when his assistant said, "Hold it. Don't hit from there, Coach. That's the ladies' tee. The men's tee is about fifty yards behind you."

John said, "Look. It took me three strokes to get here!"

When you're a sportscaster, it's very important to have as many anecdotes as possible. You can sprinkle them into your sportscast often. I began as a sportscaster and sports writer. In Los Angeles I hosted a show called "Sports Nuts with Gary Owens" on KLAC and would have the biggest sports stars on for interviews. Norm Epstein was manager of KLAC 570 at the time and, to this day, has more fantastic sports memorabilia than anyone I know—a bat belonging to Babe Ruth, a Lou Gehrig glove, and a baseball that once hit Herbert Lenfesty in the forehead. I took over the show from the splendid comedian Gabe Kaplan, star of TV's "Welcome Back Kotter," and it was pure sports presentation with facts, theories, and humor.

Top Sports-Announcing Goofs of All Time

What you say and how you say it as a sports announcer can severely affect not only the quality of your broadcast but also your professional reputation. Therefore, it's very important to think before you speak, instead of the other way around. Naturally, due to the fast-paced nature, now and then every announcer encounters a slip of the tongue or mixes metaphors in a way that ends up becoming a classic spoof, goof, flub, or blunder. Here's my list of top sports-announcing goofs of all time:

- During the course of an auto race, announcer Murray Walker made a curious comment: "The most important part of the car," he declared, "is the nut that holds the wheel."

- Sportscaster Curt Gowdy, recapping the final score of an All-Star Baseball Game: "And at the game's end, it's National League 6, American League 4," he declared. "The score again is American League 6 and National League 4."

- British sports commentator David Coleman, describing track star Moses Kiptanui during an important meet: "And here's Moses Kiptanui, the nineteen-year-old Kenyan who turned twenty a few weeks ago."

- San Diego Padres announcer Jerry Coleman, known for more than his share of on-air bloopers, calling a remarkable baseball play: "Winfield goes back to the wall. . . . He hits his head on the wall, and it rolls off! It's rolling all the way back to second base! This is a terrible thing for the Padres!"

- A sportscaster calling the action after Ralph Sampson missed a left-handed hook shot: "Well, I guess we can see that Ralph Sampson isn't a left-handed hooker."

- An announcer commenting on the location of America's Cup racing: "It's an island because it's surrounded by land. I mean water. Islands are surrounded by water, and that affects them."

- Legendary baseball announcer Hank Greenwald, announcing that a doubleheader had been canceled due to rain: "Kansas City and Cleveland, a doubleheader, was postponed because of rain. They'll play four tomorrow."

- The late St. Louis Cardinals baseball announcer Frankie Frisch announcing the start of the game: "It's a beautiful day for a night game."

- Baseball legend Dizzy Dean, broadcasting a game on CBS Television: "I don't know how our folks come off callin' this the 'Game of the Week.' There's a much better game—Dodgers and Giants—over on NBC."

Talking Sports

Being a sportscaster gives you the opportunity to follow in the footsteps of many great announcers. Many classic broadcasts have been filled with tension, excitement, and drama. What makes for a classic is not what is said, but how you call the game and create the visual for your audience at home. In writing this book, I have reacquainted myself with many great sportscasters I have known over the years. Many of them have been behind some of the greatest sports moments in history and contributed broadcasts that were equally memorable.

The late Chick Hearn, the Basketball Hall of Fame voice of the Los Angeles Lakers, was a master at creating phrases for NBA basketball, including "He fakes him into the popcorn machine" and, for an ego-centered player who lost the ball, "The mustard is off the hot dog."

With so many wonderful sportscasters in the business, it's difficult to pick just one announcer who provided what I would call an example of a classic sports broadcast. But if someone said I had to choose, perhaps no greater example of this was Baseball Hall of Fame broadcaster Vin Scully's 1965 radio call of Sandy Koufax's perfect game, which went down in history as one of the classic sports broadcasts of all time. It was a magical moment, poetry in motion, as Vinny called the action without a script but with words that powerfully described the drama and excitement of every pitch, every strike, and every out as the game drew to a close:

Sandy's fussing . . . looks to get his sign . . . o and 2 to Amalfi-tano . . . the strike two pitch to Joe . . . fastball, swung on and missed, strike three!

He is one out away from the Promised Land . . . and Harvey Kuenn is batting for Bob Hendley. . . . The time on the scoreboard is 9:44 . . . the date September the ninth, 1965, . . . and Koufax working on veteran Harvey Kuenn.

Sandy into his windup . . . and the pitch . . . fastball for a strike! . . . He has struck out, by the way, five consecutive batters . . . and that's gone unnoticed.

Sandy ready, and the strike one pitch . . . veeerrry high . . . and he lost his hat. . . . He really forced that one. . . . That's only the second time tonight where I have had the feeling that Sandy threw instead of pitched . . . trying to get that little extra, . . . and that time he tried so hard his hat fell off. . . . He took an extremely long stride to the plate, and [catcher Jeff] Torborg had to go up to get it.

One and 1 to Harvey Kuenn . . . fastball high . . . ball two. . . . You can't blame a man for pushing just a little bit now.

Sandy backs off, mops his forehead, . . . runs his left index finger along his forehead, . . . dries it off on his left pants leg . . . all the while Kuenn just waiting.

Now Sandy looks in . . . into his windup, and the 2–1 pitch to Kuenn . . . swung on and missed! . . . Strike two!

It's 9:46 P.M., 2 and 2 to Harvey Kuenn . . . one strike away . . . Sandy into his windup. . . . Here's the pitch. . . . Swung on and missed! A perfect game!

Of course, many play-by-play announcers in sports today not only call the game but do pregame or postgame interviews with coaches and players. As a sportscaster, you have to be up for the task, and it's important to be skilled in handling a variety of personalities and egos. I've interviewed hundreds of sports personalities over the years, and if I can impart any words of wisdom on the subject of interviewing sports figures, it would be the following: Always have a plan B.

Because you may have an important guest on your show, you should always prepare for the unexpected. For many years, KMPC was the flagship station for the Los Angeles Rams, and I would broadcast before every Rams home game from the L.A. Coliseum. I would do my 3:00 to 6:00

P.M. DJ program and talk to special sports guests during my show. One week Howard Cosell was in town to do "Monday Night Football" and agreed to be interviewed. The Rams were playing the Washington Redskins that day. Howard had just written a book, and he loved the idea that he could plug it. Howard, my engineer Wayne DuBois, and I were in the broadcast booth.

At the start of the broadcast, I said, "Howard, congratulations on your new book. I read it. It's wonderful." He started talking about a few things, and I queried, "You're a former barrister? You were a lawyer?"

Howard replied, "Yes. I was." I said, "You've probably never been stumped for an answer because you're so loquacious and verbose." He laughed. "No, I never have and probably never will be."

I said, "Well, that's good, because I have to go to the bathroom. Will you take over for me?"

I ran out of the booth purposely and closed the door behind me. I planned to wait for maybe a minute to see what he would do, then go back inside. But I couldn't. The door was locked. It was three o'clock in the afternoon, and I couldn't find anyone to help, not even a security guard. I hollered, "Security. Anybody. Get me back in the studio." The whole time, Howard kept talking. I could hear him from outside the door on the loudspeaker.

One guy responded to my frantic plea and said the person who had the key to the studio was down in the Rams' locker room, and I would have to go down there to get it. I hurried as fast as I could descend from the upper level to the lower level, and Cosell kept babbling on. By the time I retrieved the key and got back to the press box, my engineer had his hands up in the air. Howard had talked twenty-six minutes nonstop, and when I unlocked the door, he was saying, "And that's the difference between George Allen of the Washington Redskins and George Allen of the L.A. Rams. Owens, that's it. I'm leaving. Good-bye."

After that experience, I never left the broadcast booth without taking a key.

7

"From Beautiful Downtown Burbank"

Announcing on Television

FROM THE DON Pardos to the Ed McMahons to the Art Gilmores and John Harlans of the world, television announcers come in all shapes and sizes . . . and all voices. Some are on-camera types who introduce shows and specials, individual segments, or the featured talent. Others are off-camera announcers, invisible to the audience and voicing countless television series and specials. Still others are booth announcers, whose powerful voices tell you what station you are watching or announce station cutaways. Even others are voices behind attention-getting promos for the latest miniseries or show on your favorite network. All have a place in the fabulous multiplex of television announcing. John Rappaport, the producer of "M*A*S*H," was once a booth announcer at Channel 13 KCOP-TV.

This type of work can bring great joy to your life, not to mention a nice standard of living. Speaking from experience, I have found it to be most rewarding and fulfilling.

I have appeared as a regular, as announcer, host, or performer, on sixteen television series and have hosted my own network television specials, including "The Gary Owens All-Nonsense News Network." I've served as the announcer for the "Rosie O'Donnell Show" and "America's Funniest Videos"; was a comedy voice for ABC Television for fifteen years, doing promos for the network's sitcoms and "TGIF" comedy night; and was the promotional announcer for "Home Improvement" and "Roseanne" for syndication. I've done promos for CBS, NBC, ABC, Fox, TBS, Warner Brothers TV, and UPN for a variety of shows.

I have also guest-starred in thousands of episodic television programs, including "The Munsters," "McHale's Navy," "I Dream of Jeannie," "Mad About You," "Sabrina the Teenage Witch," "Night Court," "Battlestar Galactica," and "That '70s Show," and served as the original host of "The Gong Show." I've also guest-starred on numerous television specials, including those hosted by Lucille Ball, Johnny Carson, Bob Hope, the Jackson Five, Henry Mancini, Dinah Shore, the Supremes, the Temptations, and many more. For years, I also served as the announcer for television's "The Wonderful World of Disney," "Bewitched," "Comic Relief," the American Comedy Awards (fifteen years), the Emmys, and the Grammys (and hosted with Bill Cosby). In 1998 Nick at Nite's TV Land selected me as their favorite TV announcer, with 59 percent of the vote in a nationwide poll.

Certainly, the greatest of all my television achievements, for obvious reasons, would have to be my time as the on-camera announcer I played on "Rowan and Martin's Laugh-In." Without "Laugh-In," I probably would never have had the enormous volume of work I have accumulated over the years for which I profusely thank George Schlatter and Ed Friendly and Dan Rowan and Dick Martin. How I became the announcer of "Laugh-In" bears noting. It illustrates the power of the media, the way one medium influences another, and the fact that you never know who's paying attention to your talent.

On my afternoon radio show at KMPC in Hollywood, I would often do silly bits, and as noted earlier, many producers would tune in and listen. An example of one crazy bit I did was a parody of "Hollywood Squares." I played the part of Peter Marshall, the original host. In the top row I had Dom DeLuise, Kate Smith, and Orson Welles. You'd hear the creaking of all the boxes beginning to break, crushing the people below. Bill Armstrong, who was producing "Hollywood Squares," phoned me and said he loved it. George Schlatter also was a fan of my radio show. I'd get

You never know who is paying attention to your talent. Fortunately for me, casting director for Universal Joe Reich liked my radio show so much he hired me to appear in several sitcoms, including one opposite a giant green man with bolts coming out of both sides of his neck. Here I'm with Fred Gwynn as Herman Munster from "The Munsters."

notes from him, or he'd call me and say, "Hey, that was a funny bit." We had never met, but he hired me without an audition for "Laugh-In." Arte Johnson and I had worked together before, and we had both been hired for the series, but they weren't exactly sure what I was going to do. One day, we had a meeting at George's office, right across the street from the Smoke House Restaurant. We ambled over there to wash the typewriter

Courtesy: NBC.

Working as a TV announcer can bring great joy to your life and the chance to be funny in another dimension. Here's the original cast of "Rowan and Martin's Laugh-In": (on the tricycle) Arte Johnson, (front row) Ruth Buzzi, Dan Rowan, Dick Martin, Goldie Hawn, (second row) Henry Gibson, Judy Carne, me, Pamela Rogers, Byron Gilliam, (back row) Teresa Graves, Jeremy Lloyd, Jo Anne Worley, and Alan Sues.

ribbon ink off our hands—we'd been writing jokes. We went into the restroom, which was made of ceramic tile, and I put my hand over my ear, imitating announcers out of the forties and fifties: "My, the acoustics are good in here." George laughed and loved it. "That's what I want you to do. Be that announcer!" he said. So that's what I did on the show.

Because of that incident, the *Hollywood Reporter* gave the following headline to the story: "'Laugh-In' Comic Signed in Men's Room in Burbank." George thought it would be funny if I was in another dimension. The hosts, Dan Rowan and Dick Martin, would do their shtick, then Judy Carne, Goldie Hawn, Ruth Buzzi, Jo Anne Worley, Lily Tomlin, Eileen Brennan, Arte Johnson, Henry Gibson, Alan Sues, Dave Madden, and the other wonderful wackos and guest stars would perform their magic. Suddenly, I was behind the 44RCA microphone with a wall clock that had extended gloved hands that grew an inch every week.

Being a top radio personality for many years in Hollywood was like a personal billboard for me. What I did on the air every day showcased my talent. That's how I have landed many announcing, acting, and voice-over jobs through the years and why I was offered my first acting job in a major television series. Because of my authoritative style, I've played many newscasters, psychiatrists, bankers, and judges on TV, and before I knew it, I was doing countless television programs, movies, commercials, animated cartoons, and other voice-over work, all as a result of my radio show.

Certainly, the highlights for me as a television announcer have been plentiful, and my reason for recalling them is only to show you how great and wonderful this profession can be. For those seeking employment, let me just say, with a little talent and your own voice, you can make it in this business, and remember, you can push a person everywhere, except through a door that says Pull.

Your Voice Distinguishes You

When you are a television announcer, your voice is what makes your work stand out, besides that wrinkled suit you forgot to have pressed and cleaned. In this profession, it's important to develop what people in the biz call a "signature voice." It's not something you write, obviously, but it's a personal imprint you make with your voice.

Just venture into your TV set any day or night of the week, and when you watch a television special, concert, or late-night show, you'll see what I mean. My friend Jay Leno was formerly introduced nightly by the talented Edd Hall (first hired as a radio announcer in upstate New York at age fourteen), whom I have substituted for on several occasions. Edd is a good example of a top-notch announcer. He punched it up every night, introducing Jay in the opening segment with "It's the Tonight Show with Jay Leno!" Don Pardo does the same thing as the voice of "Saturday Night Live" when he intones, "Live from New York, it's 'Saturday Night Live!'" He dramatizes every word.

Even as I am writing this book, I am doing my Gary Owens voice. Sometimes people ask me, "Do you ever not talk like that?" If you wake me up in the middle of the night, I sound like actor (now California governor) Arnold Schwarzenegger. Actually, I always sound this way.

It is funny what a signature voice will do for you. Every now and then, a person will spot me someplace and say, "Oh, my God! Just a minute. I know you. You sound so familiar." I usually blush a little. Finally, they put it all together. "You're . . ." Naturally I expect to hear my name any moment. "You're the . . ." Spit it out, please. My publisher tells me this book can be only one volume. "You're the Announcer Guy. You're Gary Owens!"

You see my point. Having a signature voice that people associate as yours is worth everything in this business, even if they don't remember your name right away.

In announcing as in disc jockeying, newscasting, and sportscasting, different styles appeal to different folks, and people are hired for different things. Charles Aidman, a wonderful announcer and actor, always did a low-key voice. You probably wouldn't have hired Charles for something that was totally bombastic. Instead you'd hire someone like Don Pardo, who's up-tempo by his very nature—with his voice. So each person has a unique style.

"From beautiful downtown Burbank" was a signature phrase I coined on my radio show and later used on TV's "Rowan and Martin's Laugh-In." I had done phrases like this for many years on my radio show on KFWB and KMPC. When giving the weather forecast, I'd say, "Well, here's the forecast for Magnificent Monrovia, Romantic Reseda, and Beautiful Downtown Burbank," all suburbs of Los Angeles. When we started doing the Burbank line on "Laugh-In," it became a commonplace phrase, and it's probably one of the best-known sayings in the world.

Little did I realize the tremendous impact this gig would have on my career. Because of the enormous success of "Laugh-In," with forty million viewers tuning in every week, I have had more job offers than I could possibly count on one finger. Having the opportunity to be seen and heard and to impart my own special style of doing things and personal delivery as the on-camera announcer ("Almost live . . . from beautiful downtown Burbank") catapulted me to new heights, and fortunately I have enjoyed a long and successful career. I appeared in every episode of "Laugh-In" from the late sixties into the early seventies. Only Ruth Buzzi, the late Dan Rowan, Dick Martin, and I share that wonderful distinction. Working with all the tremendous talents on the series was like going to Comedy College.

Besides developing your own signature voice and style, three more ingredients are important for success as a television announcer: adding vocal color to what you read, maintaining energy in your voice, and fitting your tone of voice to the job.

Adding Color to Your Images

One thing about television announcing is that you really have to know what you are doing to be successful. TV announcing differs from disc jockeying and news announcing in one very big way: When using your voice, you must color the images that you are reading from a script. In other words, I may say a word like *attitude* a little differently than the next person. Or, if you're talking about "color video," there are little nuances you might inject that add to the flavor of the spot.

There are certain lines or words you may need to punch up. That's more the case with narrative lines. In television promo copy, almost all of it is an exclamatory phrase of some kind: "You'll laugh your butt off!"

Owner–agent Rita Vennari (of Sutton, Barth & Vennari) says that colorizing a phrase, whatever it is, works very well in television announcing as well as in commercials. That way you create your own individual style. You can be totally individual this way. With television announcing, you don't want too much colorization, however, because the producer or the director of the spot or show you're doing doesn't want you to be overwhelming.

If you're doing a live show, like the Motion Picture Academy, Emmy, Grammy, or American Comedy awards, you'd start out, "Live . . . from the Kodak Theatre in Hollywood . . . it's the Seventy-Fifth Annual Academy Awards," and you color those kinds of phrases with your voice. If you are doing a network promo, keep the energy level the same when saying, "Jamie Lee Curtis and Richard Lewis in *Anything but Love* tonight on ABC." It's emphatic enough that everyone gets the picture. Usually the producer of the show or spot will tell you what they want you to put into it. Even if they hire you because you're a known personality, they still will say, "Why don't you just gloss over 'Member FDIC,' because everybody knows what that is anyway."

The longer you've been around in the business and the more experience you gain in television announcing, the more you'll bring a perspective that producers are looking for and a way of phrasing they expect. You'll know how to handle a variety of situations because you've handled similar ones many times before. Sometimes you don't get a chance to think. For example, a producer may simply hand you some copy and say, "Now read this." If you read the last line, oftentimes you can get the gist of what it is they are selling, so if you don't have time to practice, just read the last line. As a beginner, you might not know everything, might not even know how you would bring color to a phrase, but you can, so long as you keep working at it.

It's important to ask yourself some questions about what you're reading before you begin announcing. Who's your audience? Who are you directing this to? Based on your answers to these questions, you can form a silent mental lead-in that is appropriate and brings you right where you want to be with the style of your voice.

An example of this is when I've done network promos and the word *next* would come up. *Next* is such a short word, so I would always say to myself, "You're right, it's coming up!" That would be my silent kind of phrase, so when I said, "next," I would make it more dramatic sounding, put greater emphasis in how I say it. This proven method has been around for many years, and it really works.

Maintaining a High-Energy Voice

Being an announcer, whether for a major television series, special, or promo, requires a tremendous amount of energy. The key is to maintain your voice at an optimum level at all times. In the case of promos, you will have to redo them several times with energy and enthusiasm. There are many ways to do this. Maintain a healthy diet, take vitamins, exercise, and eat regular meals. You should be ready to give 100 percent each time.

George Sidney, the great MGM movie director who directed many classic movies including *Bye Bye Birdie*, *The Harvey Girls*, and *Viva Las Vegas*, once told me a story that illustrates this point. George called me one day and asked me to come over to his house, saying, "I want to play something for you from my archives."

I arrived at George's house, and he took out a tape that had been cut at MGM for postproduction of a movie starring Jeanette McDonald and Nelson Eddy. The voice on the tape, which was George's, said, "OK, Jeanette. Take nine." The cameras started rolling again, and as Jeanette went into her big singing number, all you could hear in the background was a sound like the low rumble of a tractor. "Where is that noise coming from?" Nobody seemed to know. So George continued, "OK. Take ten. Quiet everybody."

Once again, Jeanette started to sing, and that noise came back. George was getting furious. Suddenly Jeanette spoke up. "George, I'm sorry."

He said, "Why?"

Jeanette said, "I think it's my fault. I didn't eat breakfast this morning, and it's my stomach growling."

Nelson Eddy started laughing so hard he fell down on the ground. Jeanette's stomach growls were being amplified into George's earphones, making that mysterious sound!

Doing a Voice That Fits

Sometimes jobs call for different types of voices—a happy or dramatic voice—and you'll need to prepare yourself to do that kind of voice at will. When announcing a happy spot or something upbeat, setting your lips as if you are smiling really helps. Smiling while doing your announcing puts your voice in a happy zone. Obviously, doing a dramatic voice comes from the way you emphasize the points of the script you are reading, raising and lowering the level of your voice as needed. It's all a game, really, only there are no losers. Everybody is a winner in this case—especially you, because you get paid.

When asked what he looks for in a promo announcer, Ryan Hedlund of CED Talent Agency had this to say:

> *Something unique, yet familiar in their read. That something that sets them apart from the rest of the pack. Promos are a highly competitive area of the voice-over business and require very specific skills. It's not always about the voice but how the announcer interprets the script and sees the world . . . he or she has to be very aware of current cultural trends. You can always tell who those announcers are that will be around for a while. They are the ones who keep an eye on trends, reinvent, and constantly work on their craft.*

Voice-Along with Gary

Have you ever seen one of those "bouncing ball" cartoons where everyone in the theater or at home sang along to words that were highlighted by a bouncing ball? Sorry, no bouncing balls are included with this book, but I do have some lovely parting gifts: sample scripts that you can try at home with your spouse or friends, or if you don't have any friends, a stranger will do.

Off-Camera Announcing

Television announcers are transition people. They start the show, do four or five segments in the middle, and usually end the program. Sometimes they do only the opening and ending. Whether you are doing on-camera or off-camera announcing, the style is virtually the same. Everything you say, you emphasize with your voice.

Many times what you have to announce will be little bursts of ideas that you have to get across quickly to the audience. For fifteen years, I was the announcer for the American Comedy Awards for ABC and Fox, and what I announced always segued into something else:

MUSIC: THEME

(OPENING MONTAGE OF ARRIVING STARS AND CLIPS FROM NOMINATED PERFORMANCES)

GARY OWENS (V.O.)

Tonight, from the Shrine Auditorium, in Los Angeles . . .

VTPB: TITLES

GARY OWENS (V.O.)

It's the Sixth Annual American Comedy Awards.

(APPLAUSE)

(OPENING MONTAGE OF STAR ARRIVALS AND NOMINATED FILM CLIPS CONTINUES WITH THE MUSIC UNDER)

MUSIC: OUT

(APPLAUSE)

(INTO: INTRO ROGER MOORE)

MUSIC: ROLL MUSIC

GARY OWENS (V.O.)

Ladies and gentlemen, Roger Moore.

(APPLAUSE)

In other cases, you may do more than announce quick, short bits and announce more substantial introductions or segues. Nonetheless, it's important to optimize what you say with your voice. When I worked as the off-camera announcer on "The Jack Sheldon Show," the opening spot called for me to talk above the theme music, as follows:

OPENING SPOT

MUSIC IN: THEME SONG

GARY OWENS

It's the Jack Sheldon Show . . . with Jack's friends . . . (in order of height) Louis Nye, Tom Poston, Bert Remsen, Jack Riley, Ross Tompkins, Arnie Kogen, and me, Gary Owens. Also, special guest appearances by movie producer Mark Rydell and film critic and author Leonard Maltin. Special music guests Pete Condoli and Bobby Troupe. And . . . the Wilfred Brimley Dancers! And now . . . Jack Sheldon.

Other times, besides doing the opening and closing of a show, you may announce different segments or guests. I played the dual role of off-camera and on-camera announcer for a live television special, "Stand Up Comics Take a Stand," which benefited United Cerebral Palsy, and had to switch from being an off-camera talent to an on-camera one:

GARY OWENS (V.O.)

And now, please welcome one of America's favorite TV psychologists, from the hit series "Cheers," Bebe Neuwirth!

(ENTER BEBE NEUWIRTH STAGE RIGHT)

BEBE NEUWIRTH

Before we introduce our next finalist, I'd like to bring someone out to join me here on stage. He's one of America's most recognizable faces and voices, our announcer tonight, Mr. Gary Owens.

(ENTER GARY OWENS STAGE LEFT, CROSSES THE PODIUM)

Courtesy: ABC.

When I was hosting "The Gong Show," my pal, "Mr. Warmth," Don Rickles surprised me as a mystery contestant, whistling the "C.P.O. Sharkey" theme through his hat!

(ONCE AT PODIUM, BOTH BEBE AND GARY PAUSE A BEAT FOR EDITING PURPOSES)

BEBE NEUWIRTH

If you haven't picked up the phone to call United Cerebral Palsy, it's time for you to do so. And it's time for us to take a moment to thank some of the many people who've made this show possible.

GARY OWENS

Thanks to the many clubs where we held our runoffs: the Improv, the Ice House, Igby's, L.A. Cabaret, the Laff Stop, and the Laugh Factory.

On-Camera Announcing

As an on-camera announcer, you enjoy the benefit of people seeing and hearing your work, and because of this, you get a chance not only to look, but also to act, the part. Depending on the nature of the program you are announcing, you can add some interest by your expressions and the nuances in your voice. The following are three examples of on-camera announcing scripts to demonstrate:

ROWAN AND MARTIN'S LAUGH-IN

(GARY OWENS IN ANNOUNCER SET)

GARY

Last week at this time, NBC presented the first in a series of television shows entitled "Rowan and Martin's Laugh-In." . . . The reaction was tremendous. In spite of this and in defiance of numerous requests, tonight NBC is once more going to Sock It to You.

LETTERS TO LAUGH-IN

(GARY ENTERS FROM TURNTABLE, TAKES HAND MIKE, GOES DOWNSTAGE)

GARY

Thank you . . . and welcome to "Letters to Laugh-In" . . . television's gamiest game show. And while our special guest, Mickey Mouse, is backstage trying to build a better MAN TRAP, I'll go ahead and introduce the funsome foursome who will read the jokes sent in by our audience.

AMERICA'S FUNNIEST VIDEOS SHOW

(BOB MAKES HIS ENTRANCE)

Courtesy: ABC/National Academy of Recording Arts and Sciences.

When you are a television announcer, your voice is what makes your work stand out. Here I am with Bill Cosby, cohosting the Grammy Awards.

GARY (V.O.)

Ladies and gentlemen, Bob Saget.

(APPLAUSE)

(BOB)

Thank you very much. You know this show is kinda like Elvis Presley. You think you see it everywhere. . . . We sighted it in malls, airports . . . and it's all because of fodder like this. . . . So reheat your corn dog and hold on to your TV tray 'cause here come some yuks . . .

GARY (V.O.)

Hey, America . . . we want to see some of the funny signs in your neighborhood. So grab your camcorder and start shooting. Send funny sign videos along with your other funny or amazing home videos to: Post Office Box 4333, Hollywood, California 90078. Write this address for full contest rules. Just think, your chance at 10,000 or maybe even 100,000 dollars is just one videotape away.

Promo Announcing

Announcing television promos can be short and sweet fifteen-second bridges used on networks designed to get the attention of viewers in a hurry. Here's an example from WTBS Superstation's Chimp Channel promotional tie-in that I did the voice-over announcing for:

TBS ON-AIR PROMOTION
CHIMP CHANNEL/THUNDER TIE-IN

SPOT 1

(CLEAR THROAT)

Attention, wrestling fans! Tonight is THE night! With the premiere of television's newest, most outrageous show! It's the Chimp Channel. Coming up right after Thunder. And it's only on the Superstation.

SPOT 2

Wrestling fans, the big event is just moments away! It's the brand-new series you'll go ape over. . . . The Chimp Channel's Big Premiere is coming up next on the Superstation. So just sit back . . . and let a network run by a bunch of monkeys take you to Ha Ha Land.

Be Ready for Anything

Now that I have sold you on the merits of becoming a television announcer, it's important to remember that, as in any trade or profession, you will experience great highs and great lows. Obviously, the highs are wonderful, and the lows are tough—especially if you are not a great limbo dancer.

To be successful as a television announcer, you should be prepared for anything. I quickly learned the importance of this, especially when doing television, whether I was announcing or acting.

In the 1980s, I cohosted and announced the "Miss Piggy Goes Hollywood" special on CBS along with Dick Van Dyke, Rita Moreno, and Johnny Mathis. I emerged onstage clad in a tuxedo, and twelve Nubian guards carried in Miss Piggy. The show was taped at the Ambassador Hotel and featured an all-star audience, a veritable who's who of famous Hollywood names in attendance.

After introducing Miss Piggy, I said, "Ladies and gentlemen, it's my pleasure to introduce your host of the evening, Kermit the Frog."

As I made the announcement, the electricity suddenly went out in the building, and everything turned pitch dark. People were fumbling around backstage, trying to see where they were going. Jim Henson, the creator of the Muppets, came up to me and said, "Gary, can you fill for forty-five minutes?" In the business, *fill* means to stretch. "It's going to take that long to restore power."

I said, "Well, probably, Jim." Actually, I had done shtick before the show. Part of my job as the announcer was to warm up the audience, so I had used up all my material and was totally unprepared to fill for forty-five minutes. Meanwhile, emergency power came on, enough to light the studio audience.

Thinking quickly, I went back onstage and said, "Ladies and gentlemen, we have a slight delay. We're not sure how long this will take, but we want you to meet some of the great stars here tonight." I introduced Dick Van Dyke again. "Dick's one of the hosts for tonight's show." Besides his film and television work, Dick had recently filmed a popular Kodak television commercial.

Courtesy: NBC.

Jack Carter salutes Jill St. John's pet lobster as Ruth Buzzi, Dick Martin, Jill and I (the host) strike a morose pose for the network TV audience.

I spotted Michael Landon. "Well, look, Michael Landon's in the audience. Michael, come up here." He also had done a Kodak commercial and was the star of the popular NBC drama "Little House on the Prairie." Then I saw James Garner, also in attendance. "Why, look, it's Jim Garner. Jim, please join us." He had done those famous Polaroid commercials with Mariette Hartley and starred in the Emmy-winning drama "The Rockford Files," also on NBC.

They all came up on stage and had *absolutely* no idea what they were doing there. So I said, "For the next few minutes, they're going to discuss the merits of their commercials that you've seen." The audience roared with laughter. I ran backstage, leaving the three of them to ad-lib for a while, while I tried to think of what I could do next. I came back out, and one tiny bulb came on, so I spent the next forty-five minutes interviewing celebrities in the audience—from Ginger Rogers, to Christopher Reeve, to Candice Bergen!

In 1983, I was a regular on the nationally syndicated, live one-hour magazine show "Breakaway," hosted by Monte Markham, Martha Lambert, and Norman Mark. As the announcer and feature reporter, I had to stand in whenever the show ran short on time. If a guest finished early, I would jump in for the last few minutes of the show and close by doing jokes about something that happened during the program. That's one thing about announcing. You never know what's around the corner.

No matter what happens around you, it's important to keep your composure. I've found this to be true many times during my career, especially when NBC hired me to announce its fall network lineup at its annual affiliates' convention, attended by general managers from every NBC station.

I interviewed stars from the networks' most popular and most promising new shows as part of a film montage that was shown to the general managers of these stations. To present its new lineup, NBC decided to use a series of prop "doors" (Door Number One, Door Number Two, Door Number Three, etc.) that I would knock on, and out would pop a famous NBC star, whom I would introduce.

Behind Door Number One would be Rock Hudson and Susan Saint James, stars of "McMillan and Wife." Behind Door Number Two would be Hugh O'Brian and Burgess Meredith, stars of the drama "Search." Behind Door Number Three would be Neville Brand of "Laredo" television fame. Neville was one of the great heroes of World War II.

I went through my spiel. I knocked on the first door. "Well, it's Rock Hudson and Susan Saint James, stars of 'McMillan and Wife.'" I kibitzed with them, and they talked about their show and how wonderful it was. Then I moved on to Door Number Two and knocked. "Well, look who we have here. It's Hugh O'Brian and Burgess Meredith." We, too, kibitzed, and they plugged their new show. Then I sauntered over to Door Number Three, where Neville Brand was supposed to be, only the door didn't open. I quickly ad-libbed, "Well, maybe Neville's gone to another door or something." An usher heard me and opened the door for Neville, who was standing there totally nude with a drink in his hand, saying, "What do you want?"

Quickly rebounding, I mustered a flustered comment: "Oh, my gosh. It's the six o'clock nudes, and those are the headlines."

The lesson here is that, if you want to be a famous television announcer, above all else, always know where the exit is.

8

The Crazy World of Commercials

IF YOU'RE NOT sure about being a radio host or a TV announcer and you know you like working in confined spaces with a microphone stuck up your nostrils, then working in commercials may be right for you. Commercials represent perhaps one of the most lucrative areas for voice artists, and you're still in a booth with a microphone. With the right opportunities and the right commercials, your income can exceed six or seven figures (as in *mucho dinero*).

The possibilities are limitless. I average about eight hundred to a thousand commercials and promo announcements a year and have voiced a cross-section of commercials for nationally known brands, products, companies, and services. I have been part of many ads that have won Clio Awards, IBA Awards, Suny Awards, and a self-sticking tattoo of Alfred E. Neuman that was supposed to fade after two days but has become permanently attached to my forehead.

Seriously, though, commercials can be a rewarding profession in so many ways. The earning potential is great, and so are the people you work with. I've crossed paths with many wonderful people in the business, all hardworking and talented toilers in the stucco vineyards of advertising.

Working in commercials provides a flexible time schedule and permits you to work at other jobs. If it's your part-time occupation, commercial spots can be a great supplemental income while you pursue additional possibilities for employment with your voice. In fact, most people in this business have not one job, but many jobs. If you are near a major city, more work can be had than if you are in a small town.

There was a period of time when actors wouldn't do commercials because they thought the overexposure would hurt their careers. Back in the 1960s, that all changed when people like Herschel Bernardi, a very good, legitimate actor, started doing them. He did voice narration for the Jolly Green Giant and Ford. By doing this, he was able to make enough money so he could act in off-Broadway theater—his passion, which didn't pay as much—and not starve to death. However, not all actors are sold on the benefits of doing commercials. Many stars today still keep a low profile by limiting their work in this field and doing commercials that are broadcast only overseas.

If you want to do this because you heard that Harrison Ford made $4 million doing Fiat, you're going into it for the wrong reason. Obviously, they paid Harrison a huge sum because he's one of Hollywood's most bankable actors and top box-office draws of all time. Love of money shouldn't be your first motive for doing anything. You have to love what you are doing—love the work first. When you love the work, it becomes fun, no matter how much you earn or whether you have to stand on a street corner holding a sign saying, "Will Voice for Food."

Your average voice artist may not be a known entity. Most would never be recognized on the street, nor be household names. But if they are lucky enough, they can make hundreds of thousands of dollars or more per year doing it. You can have a wonderful lifestyle with those kinds of earnings, and many announcers make millions of dollars a year, though this is not the norm for every commercial announcer.

If you land a national on-camera account or television spot, it pays more than radio commercials. There is a basic pay scale that varies from city to city. Once you gain experience, your agent can often negotiate a higher fee. The bigger the name, obviously, the higher the amount.

When doing commercials, you get to plug all kinds of products, such as this all-purpose detergent that removes even stubborn plaque buildup and your mouth!

If you do voice narration for a fast-food commercial or a beer commercial, most spots of this kind run an average of thirteen weeks. If it is renewed for another thirteen weeks, you are paid again. It's a lot of hard work, but then again, so is propelling yourself forward by patting yourself on the back. By the same token, if you have a good run on something or the commercial is popular and airs for some time, it will only help your career and your bank account. Unfortunately, this isn't always the case. Many commercials run only a few days. So, in some instances, you make just the initial fee. But when you get that one spot and hit a home run, it's not only a great feeling, but also ammo for your demo.

Voices for Hire in Commercials

Voice artists always in great demand are those who possess a straight announcing or personality voice. A straight announcing voice is fine for most voice-over work in commercials, both radio and television. The personality category covers character, celebrity voices, impersonations, people with well-known voices, and famous personalities doing their own voices. In some cases, a straight announcer may be all producers want. It depends on the nature of the commercial, of course. Other times a producer will prefer someone who does a personality voice to sell the message or product. Many golden-voiced announcers and broadcasters have made the transition to successfully doing radio or television commercials, too. Radio personalities have an edge to their voice, and many have been quite successful and are used a great deal. Certainly, if you are able to do both straight announcing and personality voicing, you improve your chances of getting more commercial work.

Landing Your First Commercial Job

When auditioning, you must go through a cattle call where you and fifty other people read for the same job. Usually your agent will contact you about an opportunity to audition, and it's up to you to follow through. You may feel as if you'll never win, never get the job, but you will. Confidence and persistence breed success. You have to remain confident in yourself, no matter what the outcome, and know that today could be your lucky day.

Ad agency people, casting directors, and producers are involved in deciding who is selected for commercials. Once you get a good reputation

© Hanna-Barbera Productions/Post Cereals. All rights reserved.

When doing voice-overs for commercials, you sometimes become part of the situation. That's what happened to me in this Fruity Pebbles commercial in which Fred and Barney discover that an oncoming stegosaurus has a brain the size of a pebble—but not as tasty.

in the business and they know the type and quality of work you do, you may get called back often. In preplanning meetings, the Head Someone may say, "Well, get so-and-so."

Someone Else may say, "Who's so-and-so?"

Another Person may chime in, "You know, so-and-so who does that voice of so-and-so."

The Other Person will say, "Which so-and-so is that?"

The Head Someone will say, "Whose agent is so-and-so."

Everybody in the Room will all nod at once. "Oh, that so-and-so."

Then Someone Else will concur, "But can we get so-and-so?"

The Other So-and-So, I mean, Head Someone (confusing, isn't it?), will say, "Well, call so-and-so and find out."

Someone Else—who chimed in before the Head Someone—will note, "I don't think we have so-and-so's phone number."

Finally, the Voice of Reason (the boss over the Head Someone and Everybody in the Room), who hasn't said anything yet during the meeting, will speak up. "Call so-and-so, and they can get you the phone number for so-and-so, and we can be done with this so-and-so meeting so I can keep my lunch meeting with that other so-and-so for the so-and-so campaign, and we can be finished with this so-and-so meeting before my so-and-so bladder bursts!"

It all works out in the end, and usually they do get so-and-so for their commercial. If he's not available, then they try a second so-and-so or possibly the third one on their list of so-and-sos, if that so-and-so can't do it for some so-and-so reason.

Oftentimes ad agencies will send agents the copy for the commercial, and it's up to the agents to bring in the appropriate people to read. The copy may come from an ad agency copywriter who has written the piece with a voice talent in mind. The copywriter says to his or her producer or casting people, "Get us a Gary Owens type."

Often they do one of three things:

1. Want to see if there is anybody better than Gary Owens
2. Call my agent to see if I'm available.
3. Ask, "Who's Gary Owens?" (Usually this is someone new in the business.)

Sometimes clients come in with a preconceived idea of whom they want. Your agent may ask for some insight into what they're thinking: "Give me a name of someone you'd like." This helps agents know what kind of talent to send, if they represent someone in that area who may work.

Bob Lloyd, formerly of The Voicecaster, related such a story to me. A producer wanted a great big, deep voice singing faster and faster, and he had this tongue-twisting type of thing going on. There aren't a whole lot of people who fit this type of category. "We couldn't find him what he wanted," Bob said, "and the guy replied, 'Anybody can sing; even I can sing.'" So they sent the producer a regular singer, and he got the job.

Sometimes producers find there's nothing like the original voice artist to do their commercials, rather than pale imitators. Michael Bell was the voice of Parkay margarine for many years ("Parkay!"). Apparently, Michael got into a bit of a tiff, and the agency that produced the commercial auditioned many other voices to replace him—in New York, Chicago, and Los Angeles—to no avail. They brought Michael back.

There are also times when producers really aren't sure what they are looking for, even when it's right under their noses. Some friends of mine were once auditioning for a television commercial for a famous motel chain as the voice of a "talking briefcase." The first to audition was my buddy Alan Barzman, the voice of Energizer Bunny commercials ("They keep going, and going, and going . . . "). Alan went in and, on cue, did what he thought was the voice of a briefcase. Following his audition, the producer said, "I'm sorry. You're wonderful, but you don't sound like a briefcase."

A few years later, Alan auditioned again, this time as the voice of a cockroach, for a big-name insect spray commercial. The producer watched and listened as Alan cleverly did his cockroach voice. Afterward, the producer said, "Well, you've just about got it. That's not quite the voice of a cockroach." Alan said, "Let's go over to this plant."

They walked over to the live plant in the studio. Then Barzman said, "Now we're going to wait until a real cockroach comes along, and when you hear it speak, I'll imitate it perfectly for you."

Veteran voice artist Jack Angel suffered a similar fate when he auditioned for the voice of a hamburger. After he finished auditioning, the agency producer said, "You're very close, but that's *not* the voice of a hamburger. That's the voice of a hot dog." Later Jack told me, "He would have known, since he was a hot dog." Welcome to the crazy world of commercials.

The Challenges of Working in Commercials

More than any other job using your voice, doing radio and television commercials takes a certain degree of style and finesse, not to mention remembering where your car keys are so you can get to the studio on time. Three elements make the work extremely challenging:

Courtesy: Fred Wostbrock.

One of the hardest areas of creativity is selling the product in less than a minute. Your job as announcer is to present the commercial while holding a lucky bun in your tuxedo pocket. It was an easy sell with this campaign.

1. Time is limited. The time element in a commercial is very limited. You usually have only thirty seconds to make your spiel. It's like being on the edge of a cliff with only seconds to jump—and without a parachute.

2. Get your message across. Perhaps the greatest challenge for an announcer is getting the advertising message across and selling the product in a minute or less. Very few jobs are so demanding in so little time, except, of course, bungee jumping in Antarctica.

3. There are no visuals. When doing radio spots, you have no visuals to guide you. You have to picture the scene, imagine what you're reading, what you are creating with your voice. Usually the script provides clues as to how broad you can play a character physically and emotionally. Sometimes it pays to tweak the words a little, based on what you think producers want. That tweak will bring the twinkle in your voice and put you on the right track to making your reading flourish.

Analyzing the Script

Doing commercials, like any voice-over job, takes a great deal of preparation if you are to succeed and be effective. Over the years, I have found, no matter how many commercials you have done or how long you have been in this business, following these seven tips will help you to always do your best:

1. Read the script. Read the part you'll be playing. Familiarize yourself with the dialogue, so when you read your lines, it all comes naturally.

2. Analyze the script. Understand what you are saying and what points must be emphasized. Play up the parts of the script that are important. Underline any key words in the script that you want to emphasize for dramatic effect.

3. Colorize your words. As in television announcing (see the previous chapter for more details), colorize your words. Come up with images that represent your personal interpretation—not only what you need to say, but also how you want to say it. Creating a mental picture—something that inspires you—will help bring out the right cadence in your voice.

4. Watch your transitions. Give careful thought to your transitions—when to change your tone at the end of the sentence or the middle of one. The script is yours to work with and to keep, so, if you need to, mark it up. Make any notes you want directly on the copy to indicate when to pause, stop, or switch gears, with your voice.

5. Pace yourself. Doing commercials is like a horse race: With so little time to complete your lap around the track, stay focused and don't panic. Sometimes you may need a few reads to get the timing, the tempo, and the rhythm and flow and emphasis down just right. It's like playing tennis and trying not to hit your instructor in the head with your serve.

6. Speak from the script. Stay true to the written words. Don't improvise or change anything unless the producer or casting people agree. Remember, they're your bosses, and it's always best to ask first or speak up if something isn't right!

7. Project your voice. Project your voice clearly; modulate and maintain a consistent level of energy with your voice during your read. Achieving this is easier than you think. Read with everything you've got. Give it your all every time. Pull your voice from the vast reaches of your inner soul, up from your bootstraps, through your abdomen, and draw it out. When you repeat these simple steps, the projection of your voice will come more naturally, and you won't feel as though you have to stand on your head to do it—unless, of course, you do your best work this way.

Three Kinds of Commercials

Most commercials produced today are either humorous or dramatic. Many of the commercials I voice—although by no means all of them—have a humorous bent. They are silly, yet they get the advertising message across, and they sell a lot of product. One of the hardest areas of creativity is to make a spot funny and sell the product in less than thirty seconds or one minute. Either way, funny or straight, commercials are all about selling, and there are three main types of commercials that can showcase your vocal acting talent: spokesperson commercials, slice-of-life commercials, and voice-over narrative commercials.

The Spokesperson Commercial

In a spokesperson commercial, someone is talking directly to the camera or microphone to sell a certain product. An example of this would be a Taco Bell commercial for a sizzling-hot new summer special. The announcer says, "This Friday, Taco Bell kicks off summer with thirty-nine straight hours of thirty-nine-cent tacos. This weekend you'll get the same crunchy tacos you love, filled with tasty seasoned beef, tangy cheese, and crispy lettuce for just thirty-nine cents. This crunch-fest begins Friday at 10 P.M. and ends Sunday, the twenty-seventh, at 1 P.M. So come in to Taco Bell, and get your summer rolling!"

You've always wanted to be a spokesperson? Well, me, too. That's why I got into this crazy business. But this isn't about me. This part of the book is all about you and helping you on your way to commercial riches. So I've included a sample script for you to try. Yes, you get to be your very own spokesperson. Well, I'm happy you're happy. Glad I can be of service.

Get your stopwatch ready. The following script is for a thirty-second Ponderosa Steakhouse radio commercial, originally done by yours truly. Take some time to rehearse and prepare. Maybe do a straight announcing voice, something dramatic, as if you are a great purveyor of history.

For the legendary French character François Buffet, you'll need to sound French. If you don't do a French accent very well, eating french fries while playing the French national anthem always gets me in the mood. If this fails to work, drop the accent and do your best knockoff version of a French accent, even though that Irish brogue you have may be a bit of a problem. Now, give it a whirl and make Uncle Gary proud.

ANNOUNCER

Ponderosa Steakhouse presents "The History of Great Tasting Food."

1744. François Buffet invents . . . you guessed it . . . the buffet.

FRANÇOIS (IN THICK FRENCH ACCENT)

Let them eat cake, and those cute little chicken wings!

ANNOUNCER

1998. Ponderosa reinvents the buffet with their Hearty Homestyle Lunch. With more choices than ever, like meatloaf, lasagna, and beef stew, it's probably the best-tasting lunch buffet in history. And the Hearty Homestyle Lunch Buffet is all you can eat, for one great price. So come in and . . .

SING OUT

Take another taste of Ponderosa.

The Slice-of-Life Commercial

In the case of a slice-of-life commercial, a short story, with a beginning, middle, and end, is resolved in thirty seconds, often with the announcer playing an integral part. Usually this type of commercial deals with everyday situations to which people can readily relate, like maybe a family crisis or real-life problem.

One example I announced was a Jiffy Lube radio commercial about a man who had just finalized his divorce. As the announcer, I began, "His lengthy divorce finalized, Ed Gredvig rushes to a midnight rendezvous with Rose Davino, to leave town together and begin a whole new life." Suddenly you hear the sound of a tire blowing. Thwack. Thwack. A distraught Ed says, "Flat tire! Oh, man!"

Dramatic music underscores the scene as I intone dramatically, "Her hopes having been dashed in the past, Rose has told Ed if he doesn't show by 12:15, she's calling the whole thing off." The car stops, and the door opens. Ed says, "Why me?" The car door slams. Ed struggles with his keys and opens the trunk.

Meanwhile, I announce cheerfully, "Too bad Ed didn't have his oil changed at Jiffy Lube. Where now, with a Signature Service Oil Change with Pennzoil, you also get Pennzoil Roadside Assistance, free."

The loud sound of tools rattling is heard, and Ed says angrily, "All right, where's the jack?" More rattling. "Where's the jack?" More rattling, then the trunk slams shut. Ed screams hysterically, "I ain't got a jack!"

At that moment, as the announcer, I come back and say, "Roadside help will always be there—with tire changes, jump starts, emergency gas, locksmith service, and more."

Ed dials his cell phone. We hear it ringing. "C'mon Rose, pick up, hang in there for me, baby." Music swells in the background, and I conclude, "Get free Pennzoil roadside help in a jiffy. Stop in Jiffy Lube for details. Jiffy Lube. There's no substitute for the best."

In a slice-of-life commercial, you can play a range of characters—from the announcer to real-life people—and your voice can range from dramatic to melancholy. Much of this depends on the nature of the spot, whether it is trying to be dramatic or humorous. Emote the way the spot is designed.

The following example is a finished script from a humorous radio commercial campaign I did for Round Table Pizza, called "The Adventures of Gary Garlic." Here's your chance to play a range of characters: Gary, the poor bulb of garlic who doesn't very much like dinner (especially the fact he's it); Bill, the chef who is preparing a delicious new entrée offered at Round Table Pizza; and the melancholy announcer of your very own slice-of-life commercial.

ROUND TABLE

GARY/CONVENIENCE/ADD ROASTED GARLIC OFFER
:60 RADIO

(HAPPY THEME MUSIC IN)

GARY

Hi, everybody, my name's Gary, and I'm a little bulb of garlic. Ha ha ha ha ha.

HAPPY SINGERS

The Adventures of Gary Garlic

(MUSIC OUT)

GARY

What are we doing today, Bill?

BILL

Today we're going to review some dinnertime tips.

GARY

I like dinnertime!

BILL

First, be sure and purchase ingredients ahead of time, like this twenty-pound block of cheese . . .

GARY

That's a big piece of cheese.

(SOUND EFFECT: WHAM OF CHEESE CRUSHING GARY)

GARY (MUFFLED)

. . . Ow.

BILL

Allow plenty of time to cook ingredients, like this zesty tomato sauce.

(SOUND EFFECT: HOT LIQUID GETS DUMPED ON GARY)

GARY

Whoa! I think it's done.

BILL (FAKING CONCERN)

Sorry, Gary . . .

GARY

Dinnertime is hard!!!

BILL

Dinnertime is hard. Just like this rolling pin . . .

(SOUND EFFECT: WHAM, WHAM, WHAM, WHAM, WHAM)

GARY (A BIT DISHEARTENED)

Hey!

BILL

There you have it, folks, Gary's dinnertime tips. And now a word from our sponsor.

(THEME MUSIC UP AND UNDER)

ANNOUNCER

Brought to you by the people at Round Table Pizza, who remind you that it would probably be safe, easier, and a lot more convenient to have a pizza delivered tonight. Try one with roasted garlic for a unique, new taste. Round Table. The last honest pizza.

(THEME MUSIC OVER APPLAUSE)

HAPPY SINGERS

Gary Garlic, everyone's favorite pal . . .

The Voice-Over Narrative Commercial

Last but not least, the voice-over narrative commercial is one of the most widely produced types of commercials in the business. A voice actor off-camera or behind the microphone narrates a situation—maybe a house-wife who is looking into the mirror and thinking how she looks. The voice tells her—instead of how she *really* looks—what brand of shampoo to use.

Another situation might be something like buying the best cell phone. For Alltel, I was the voice-over announcer for a major radio cam-paign featuring the famous comic strip character Dick Tracy. Following a short music intro, I set up the situation through snappy voice-over narra-tion: "Alltel and Dick Tracy in (*Music flourishes*) 'Wake Up and Smell the Future.' We join Tracy tied to a chair in a deserted warehouse. The Brow approaches."

Brow drops by to see Tracy shoot some pool and, in conversation, notices Tracy has something behind his back that isn't his famous wrist radio. It's his new digital cellular phone from Alltel. After Tracy demon-strates some of the phone's many outstanding features, including caller ID, I conclude, "Sign up now for Alltel's new digital cellular service, and you'll get more digital minutes per month for a year. Digital clarity, nation-wide cellular coverage. Come in or call 1-800 . . . See stores for details. Some restrictions apply."

Sounds pretty easy, doesn't it? Well, it is. Being a stylized narrator is a lot of fun. You get to voice many different commercials that call for this special talent. As in the case of audiobooks or feature films, the purpose of the narrator is to move the story along and to sell the product.

Get your sales shoes on and that pitch in your voice. You get to be the narrator for Mattel Games' "Ways to Play Uno" television commer-cial—unless being Yukky Lady is your thing. Oh, heck, why not? It's your career. Of course, since this script calls for so many other voices, you may want to call a few friends to help, especially someone to play Huge Guy . . . which is a lot better part than Yukky Lady (just don't tell her).

MATTEL GAMES

WAYS TO PLAY UNO
:30 TV

SINGERS

Do U Know Uno?

GARY OWENS (V.O.)

There are hundreds of ways to play Uno. . . . In Cleveland they play Zero Uno!

YUKKY LADY

Uno!

(GUY WITH TONS AND TONS OF CARDS PLAYS A ZERO)

GUY

Zero. You gotta change hands!

YUKKY LADY

Nohhhh!!

(DOG SNARLS)

GARY OWENS (V.O.)

In Tampa Bay, it's No-Whining Uno . . .

HUGE GUY

Aww, come on, guys! No, pleeeez!

ALL

No whining allowed! Draw three more.

GARY OWENS (V.O.)

It's Snow Uno in Idaho. The winner must take a victory lap. Barefoot.

KIDS

Thatta girl, Yamma! Uno!

GARY OWENS (V.O.)

How do you play Uno? In Tulsa, it's Add-On Uno.

Courtesy: Fred Wostbrock

In some cases, you sell not only the product but also yourself, as I was doing in this McDonald's commercial offering a puppet that looked like me.

SIS

Draw two! Hah!

GARY OWENS (V.O.)

If you have the same draw card as the one played . . .

DAD

Draw four . . .

GARY OWENS (V.O.)

You can add on and pass it to the next guy.

MOM

Draw six!

BRO

Back to you. Draw eight, Little Sister!!!

It's All in How You Sell It

More important than the content of the commercials is the way you present them. As an announcer or voice-over talent, you're like a major-league pitcher. Sometimes the pitch you throw is fast and hard; other times it's nice and soft. Obviously, there is a major difference between the two approaches.

The Hard-Sell Commercial

A commercial with a hard sell aggressively urges those watching or listening to purchase the product immediately. Usually hard-sell spots are designed to get the audience to act right away, due to circumstances behind the product or service they are pitching. The late great Phil Hartman and I were hired to do radio commercials for Imperial Oil's $10,000-a-Day Give-Away campaign. I was the voice-over announcer; Phil played the character Bob from Esso Oil. Right away, following the musical introduction, Bob's character gets to the heart of the pitch: "Bob Velour here for the Esso $10,000-a-Day Give-Away. Every time you swipe your Esso Extra Card, you're automatically entered for a chance to win an extra $10,000 for the summer. A new winner every day in July! That's thirty-one prizes in all."

The entire spot focuses on Bob and the offer he is pushing: "I asked one of the people from our Esso Extra Department why we didn't go with February. I mean, if you're giving away money every day, why not pick a cheaper month? And she said, 'Bob, that's why you're not the announcer.'"

After a thoughtful pause, Bob makes his final push: "Because of this month, one of thirty-one $10,000 cash prizes could be yours. It's another Esso Extra, just for you, when you swipe your Esso Extra Card. See rules at participating Esso stations. Contest closes midnight, July 31. No purchase necessary, but . . . where do you think you're going this summer without gas? Huh?"

The Soft-Sell Commercial

In a soft sell, the commercial demonstrates the many distinct advantages of the product or service you're selling without demanding that people buy it. A case in point is a commercial that promotes the latest Sony VAIO personal computer. The opening pushes the product without a hard sales pitch: "How the Sony VAIO Microtower helped save flight 831." The commercial segues into the story and, between occasional narration, demonstrates the advantages of this new high-speed PC, with the characters in the story slowly becoming impressed. Finally, after it becomes apparent this is the computer to buy, I conclude in the same soft-sell approach: "To buy the Trinitron multimedia monitor and new Sony VAIO Microtower with the Intel Celeron and Pentium II processors, visit your nearest Circuit City. Act now and receive up to $225 in rebates from Sony. Purchase requirements and restrictions apply."

Commercials Are a Funny Business

Sometimes it's hard to keep a straight face when doing commercials, especially on camera. In this case, it's best to "don't worry, be happy."

A favorite story of mine involved a friend, Sam Benson, who used to do on-camera commercials for most of the local independent TV stations. He was a good spokesman for many, many years. For one particular local car dealership, Sam used to come out dressed as a magician and carrying a magician's hat from which you'd see the ears of a beautiful bunny sticking out. Sam would say, "Yes, there's magic going on at [blank-blank] car dealers," while pulling the rabbit out of the hat. They would flash the phone number on the screen. Sam would continue, "Give them a call today, and they will quote you a great price on this brand-new [whatever it was he was selling]."

After this, Sam proceeded to make his final pitch as he put the hat back on. The rabbit decided to ad-lib. (Perhaps he wasn't being paid scale.) He tinkled on Sam's head, live, on local television. Sam didn't miss a beat: "Yes, magic happens all the time at [blank-blank] car dealers," as rabbit tinkle was still streaming down his face. "Come down and see for yourself."

So the commercial business, like any business, isn't perfect. But when everything goes right, it's one of the best professions you can possibly choose.

9

Finding Fame and Fortune in Animated Cartoons

THE FIELD OF animated cartoons is especially rewarding if you have the ability to do many different voices. As with doing voice-overs in commercials, there is an opportunity to use not only your voice but your imagination as well.

Doing cartoons offers remarkable earning potential. One can make a fortune in this area, given the right situation. (Remember, the people who do the voices of "The Simpsons" each earn more than a million dollars.) That's why so many famous stars are getting into the field today. Also, doing voice work is a welcome relief. You don't have to wear makeup or get a facelift.

The latest trend in the field today is to cast major movie stars to voice animated characters—Robin Williams in *Aladdin*, Tom Hanks in *Toy Story*, Eddie Murphy in *Shrek*, Woody Allen in *Antz*, among others. Many radio personalities, broadcasters, newscasters, and announcers have also made the transition to doing cartoon voice-overs—and quite successfully, I might add.

© Spumco Company. All rights reserved.

Working in animated cartoons allows you to be cast as unusual characters that often become cult favorites, like the character Powdered Toast Man, which I played in "The Ren and Stimpy Show," created by John Krisfaluci.

Despite the proliferation of star-driven properties in Hollywood today, animation has opportunities for anyone who can do original voices, whether you do one or many. There are still plenty of voice actors who pull in a regular paycheck working on cartoons, many whose faces may not be immediately recognized, even if their voices are. Some of the most successful artists don't work exclusively in this arena. For many people, animation voice work encompasses doing other things in addition to cartoons—film dubbing, radio commercials, and television commercials, to name but a few.

Animation is one of the few businesses where you can keep on making money for your performance even after its original broadcast. Like actors in a major television series or special, you are paid not only for the first time you make the cartoon but also for up to seven reruns of the same episode. You can make an average of $750 an episode and end up making thousands over the length of the run. That means if you did twenty episodes, you would make over $15,000 for your basic pay. Then you'd be paid on the rerun, so you'd make half the original amount. Then you're paid a third on the next rerun and so forth—extra earning power, which is like frosting on the cake.

The Key to Success: Mastering Many Voices

In the world of cartoons, your ability to do many different voices can make you more valuable. If you have a repertoire—and you do them all very well—you stand a good chance of working with great regularity. Of course, this doesn't mean you can't be successful with one voice. I've made a wonderful living doing animated cartoons with primarily the same voice. I usually play the superhero or narrator, although I have done a lot of villains over the years.

I was seduced by the fantasy of cartoons and comic books at an early age. An example: When I was about eight, I used my mother's pinking shears to fashion a Superman cape from my sister Adeline's blue silk prom dress. I was so certain I could fly with this cape that I jumped off the roof. Fortunately, bushes cushioned my leap—and I lived, bruised but wiser. Being the wonderful sister she was, in a great moment of forgiveness, Adeline locked me in the cellar and told my parents I had been stolen by Gypsies.

When I was twelve years old, I won an art scholarship. It was a correspondence course. I had always loved to draw. It was escapism for me (I was quite ill from diabetes, which I have had since I was eight years old) and enabled me to inhabit fantasy worlds.

The man who chose my drawing was a guy who would later go on to be the top cartoonist in the world, the late Charles "Sparky" Schulz, creator of the popular "Peanuts" comic strip. I took his suggestions for drawing to heart and later drew the cartoons for my high school and college newspapers. I also supplemented my income for many years by selling cartoons to national magazines and the local newspaper. I later got to know Sparky quite well when we were living in San Francisco and were

© 1993 Hero Entertainment. Courtesy: Blake Snyder.

Doing one or many voices, you can enjoy tremendous success in animated cartoons. Possessing the superpower of twenty atom bombs can also help, as when I played the bravado superhero Roger Ramjet, my first animated cartoon series.

both members of the Northern California Cartoon Society. I am now a member of CAPS, the Southern California group, and the National Cartoonists Society (NCS), the group that gives the Reuben Award. David Folkman, the historian of NCS, has so much memorabilia you'll plotz. He displays many items at CAPS meetings.

My very first cartoon series as a voice actor was "Roger Ramjet" in the 1960s. Ramjet was a bravado superhero who possessed the power of twenty atom bombs for twenty seconds.

The "Ramjet" cast was great. It featured Gene Moss and Jim Thurman, later of "Sesame Street"; David Ketchum of "Get Smart"; Bob Arbogast (who created "The Question Man" for Steve Allen and "A Song Is Born" for Garry Moore); Joan Gerber, one of the top voices in Hollywood; Dick Beals, who was a regular on "The Lone Ranger" and the voice of Speedy Alka Seltzer; and Paul Shively, who did a superb Cary Grant. We also had a great assortment of guest voices, including Leon Russell and Sammy Davis Jr. The wacky nature of the series was evident even by the episode titles — "Long Joan Silver," "The Treasure in Sierra's Mattress," "The Werewolf of Lompoc."

Playing superheroes has been lucrative for me. I had been doing promos for all of the Hanna-Barbera shows when Joe Barbera and Fred Silverman, head of CBS Television, requested me for their new series, "Space Ghost and Dino Boy," featuring a unique superhero designed by the great cartoonist Alex Toth. I voiced the lead character, working along with the talented Tim Matthieson (now famous for *Animal House* and his vice presidential role on "West Wing") as Jace, Ginny Tyler as Jan, and Don Messick as Blip the Monkey.

I worked with the multitalented Daws Butler in several series, including "Scooby's All-Star Laff-a-Lympics" and "Yogi's Space Race." Daws probably did as many cartoons as you have seen — such memorable characters as Yogi Bear, Huckleberry Hound, Snagglepuss, Waldo (on "Mr. Magoo," the cartoon series), just to name a few of the hundreds.

In the 1970s, Hanna-Barbera cast me again as the superhero, Blue Falcon, in the series "Blue Falcon and Dynomutt," part of Saturday morning's "The Scooby-Doo/Dynomutt Hour." This time I played a comedic superhero alongside gifted costar Frank Welker (one of the busiest cartoon voices), who played a robotic dog, Dynomutt. Larry McCormick, a longtime expert newscaster for KTLA–Channel 5 in Los Angeles, played a role fashioned after then-mayor Tom Bradley. More recently, one of the most unusual superheroes I ever played was Powdered Toast Man on the hit cartoon series "The Ren and Stimpy Show," created by John Krisfaluci. Billy West did Ren and Stimpy, and Frank Zappa played the Pope! Powdered Toast Man was famous for shooting raisins out of his armpits at evildoers.

On many series, I have played the part of the narrator, as I did on the "Perils of Penelope Pitstop" (with Janet Waldo as Penelope), another Hanna-Barbera animated program and a fun time for all, plus many wonderful cartoon shows, too many to mention. I've also had the narrator's part on "Bobby's World," and where I played Captain Squash; Jim Davis's "Garfield and Friends," which was produced and written by Mark Evanier (he wrote every episode — an amazing feat for one person); "The Mighty Orbots"; "Legends of the Super Heroes"; "Yogi's Space Race"; "Captain Caveman"; "Scooby's All-Star Laff-a-Lympics"; and, recently for Walt Dis-

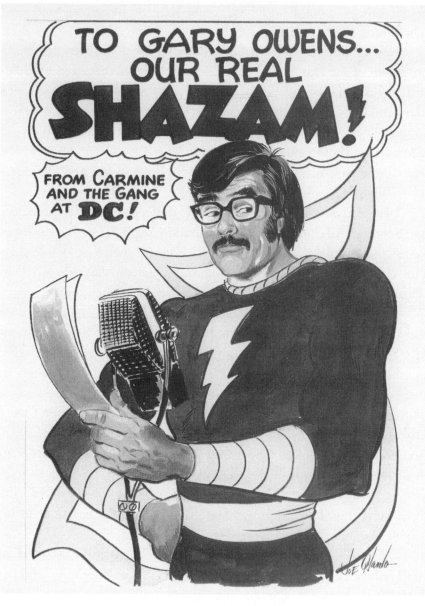

Cartooning and animated cartoons have both been a big part of my life. One childhood favorite of mine was Captain Marvel. After I mentioned this to Matty Simmons of *National Lampoon* and Carmine Infantino, the fabulous cartoonist and head of DC Publications, they surprised me with this rendering of me "shazamming" my way behind a microphone, drawn by the great Joe Orlando.

ney, "Buzz Lightyear," the TV series. I'm currently playing the announcer on a new series, "The Alan Brady Show," created and written by Carl Reiner for TV Land with TV legends Carl, Dick Van Dyke, and Rose Marie. So basically, by doing voices, I have enjoyed employment in a variety of series and numerous roles. Incidentally, I have been with "Sesame Street"—the most honored children's television show—since its inception. I was also one of the conceptual people for "The Electric Company," where Morgan Freeman got his start!

Because of my voice-over work in animated cartoons, I've been fortunate to become friends with so many of my heroes in the cartoon world: Jack Kilby, Milton Caniff, B. Kliban, Mel Lazarus, Mark Evanier, Walt Disney, Walter Lantz, Bill Keane, Al Hirshfeld, Scott Shaw, Will Eisner, Paul Conrad, Mike Kazaleh, Don Rico, Cathy Guisewhite, Darryl McNeil, and Alex Toth. I once spent an entire evening with Gary Larson of "The Far Side" comic strip. Sergio Aragones of *Mad Magazine* is a great chum, whom I see at least once a month.

One thing to keep in mind about doing voice for cartoons is that you don't have to do voice imitations of famous people to be in demand. Doing voices of regular people like a police officer, housewife, or farmer will increase your chances of employment because you bring a broader skill set to the table. Other voice artists are hired and rehired because they can do certain sounds. Usually they don't hire you because you do just one sound. But if you do lots of sounds, like different animals—a hawk, birds, prehistoric animals—then you make yourself more employable.

Many people think that, besides doing different voices, being a good artist also is necessary. That's not necessarily so, unless you want to be an animator. Animation is an entirely different department. The voice track is done first, and then artists draw characters to match the audio.

Making People Believe

The whole purpose of doing animated cartoons is to pull people into make-believe. To accomplish that, your voice or voices must be believable, too. Many popular characters—Bugs Bunny, Mickey Mouse, and the Powerpuff Girls—succeed because they all have believable voices as well as believable characters.

In doing this kind of work, you have to think and act like the character and reflect those nuances and feelings in your rendition. Mel Blanc was undoubtedly the greatest voice person of the twentieth century. As longtime friend and agent Don Pitts has said, "Mel wrote the blueprint for voice characterization for the cartoon world." He was an incredible talent whose expressions and characterizations were irrefutably unique and who brought life to Warner Brothers' favorites the world over, including Bugs Bunny, Porky Pig, Daffy Duck, Speedy Gonzales, Foghorn Leghorn, Pepe Le Pew, Sylvester, Tweety, Yosemite Sam, Wile E. Coyote, the Road Runner, and many others.

The secret to Mel's success was perhaps that he could do tricks with his voice that most people couldn't. He started out as a singer and was basically a vocalist with tremendous range. When Mel would intone his characters' voices, he would use body language and a kaleidoscope of expressions—raising an eyebrow here, twisting a lip there. He was a kind and gentle guy whose talent was gargantuan; he was the only man who could master the sound of a rubber band orally!

Those of us in the cartoon biz owe a great debt of gratitude to Mel, because one year he asked Warner Brothers cartoon producer Leon Schlesinger for a raise, and Leon turned him down (tightfisted rascal that he was). However, Mel said, "Well, then maybe I could at least get my name on the credits." No voice performer had done that, and Schlesinger agreed. It brought fame to Mel to the tune of fourteen transcontinental radio shows a week and paved the way for all us to get recognition for our labors.

Lorenzo Music is another example of a fine voice actor who didn't do a lot of voices but became extremely successful doing what he did. Lorenzo was a good pal of mine. I was the announcer on the "Garfield and Friends" animated series for years—thanks to Mark Evanier and Jim Davis—and Lorenzo was the voice of Garfield. He had this wonderful, nonplussed style, and he was also a very famous TV producer with such hit series as "Rhoda" and "The Lou Grant Show." Yet his Garfield voice was so good and interesting.

Making people believe is the whole purpose of doing animated cartoons. Mel Blanc was a master at thinking and acting like the characters he played and was undoubtedly the greatest cartoon voice person ever.

To follow in the footsteps of Mel Blanc and these other greats in the business by developing great, believable cartoon voices involves five important tips:

1. Make your voices clearly understandable. Creating characterizations that are understood by everyone is very important. As great as Mel Blanc was, you always knew the voice was Mel. His characters were so understandable because he enunciated in a marvelous way. Even when he had to stutter like Porky Pig, you knew what he was saying.

2. Consistently maintain your characterizations. The second most important practice is to keep your characterization consistent without fail. Having strong vocal chords or developing them will help you phys-

Courtesy: Jim Davis and Film Roman Productions. © United Feature Syndicate.

Some cartoon voice-over jobs are more lucrative than others. When I played the announcer in "Garfield and Friends," saying just one line worked into a wonderful eight-year gig on CBS Television. The cartoon is still running in syndication.

ically in this regard. Many cartoon voice artists get hoarse just from the strain of doing the work, because they're constantly pushing and elevating their voice to perform at a very high level of energy. Spending four straight hours and maybe twenty takes in a row saying the same thing creates a tremendous strain. So your voice must be strong.

3. Establish a separation of characters. If you do many different voices, your ability to maintain different characters at the snap of a finger also is important. You should be able to switch gears in a nanosecond, using your voice to shift among whatever characters you've been hired to play.

4. Be an actor. Voice artists are really actors with one major difference: They convey the expressions and nuances only with their voice. All of the feeling has to come through what you are saying. Cartoon voices are recorded before character drawings are done, and the drawings are matched to the voices. Therefore, the process of recording a cartoon is much different from acting in a live or filmed production, where you get into the role and play off each other's character and performance. You cannot overlap as you do in a play or a movie.

5. **Be ready to deliver.** Your success depends on your ability to deliver when called to action, whether to an audition or a job. So like the NASCAR racer, be ready to "start your engine" and deliver another peak performance.

Casting Animated Cartoons

Casting for animated cartoons is like casting for commercials. The casting director of the production studio will audition actors for different parts in an animated series, special, or feature film. Casting calls go out to the different talent agencies that represent voice-over people. Each agency is given drawings or sketches of what the character looks like, along with the following type of information: "We're looking for this character who puffs a cigar. He's very slow. He's like a tortoise. What kind of voice can you give this?"

Each voice person figures out what to sound like. Sometimes a character is created with a specific actor in mind. I believe I didn't audition for Blue Falcon because I had already done two or three other superheroes in the same genre, so they already knew what I could do.

Even if you have done thousands of cartoons, sometimes you still have to audition. Being known helps but is no guarantee for employment. With casting people changing jobs, changing studios, and generally moving around, sometimes newcomers to the business still have to learn what you can do.

Stan Freberg and June Foray, two icons in the field of animation, were sent to audition for an animated feature. When Stan asked for the directions to the studio, he was told to step across the office and read his lines into a boom box on a shelf. Moments later, an animator rounded the corner and said to Freberg, "Stan, I heard your voice coming up the hall and just wanted to say hello." The casting person, with an amazed look on her face, said to Stan, "Goodness. I'm surprised that he recognized your voice. You must do a lot of this kind of work."

Sometimes talent can put their agents in an embarrassing position as well. Years ago, at the height of his long career, the multitalented Paul Frees—a favorite voice artist with the Disney folks—was asked to report to the studio to work on one of Disney's top new animated features. His agent asked for and got Paul's usual fee at the time—$1,250 for a half day's work.

On the day he was to report to work, Paul called from somewhere on Hollywood Boulevard, claiming he had been banned from the studio and was so upset he was going to a movie. Actually, there was a new guard working the gate that day, and Paul wasn't on the list. About that time, the studio called to ask where he was. The agent told them the story, and they were furious. "Why didn't Paul have the guard call in?" the casting director asked. "Everyone on the Disney lot knows him" (except for the guard, of course). The agent took quite a tongue lashing on the phone, and rightly so.

In some cases, what the voice producers have in mind might be inappropriate for a particular character. When the marvelous people at DIC Enterprises produced the original "Inspector Gadget" animated cartoon series, Jesse White was the first person hired for the character. But they didn't think he fit. So they asked me to read for one episode, and I said, "You really want a Don Adams kind of voice." At that time Don was best known as TV's Maxwell Smart in the popular comedy "Get Smart," and he also was the voice of the character Tennessee Tuxedo, the penguin, in the cartoon by the same name.

They said, "Well, but it would be too expensive to get Don."

I said, "I think he'd love to do it." They called his agent, and, sure enough, the part of Inspector Gadget became a whole new career for him. Incidentally, Andy Heyward, the owner of DIC, and Marsha Goodman, producer, are two of my best friends. They have created some fantastic cartoons.

Recording Your First Cartoon

A normal cartoon-recording session involves reviewing scripts, recording dialogue, and general bedlam that can prevail when a group of creative, fertile minds gather together in one tiny recording studio. The sessions can be lots of fun, with people kidding around and recording material that could never be aired.

When doing voice-overs for cartoons, you never see the cartoon until after the audio is added. (The voices and animation are matched later after animators have drawn all the "cels," or scenes of characters and backgrounds.) For the most part, you know what the characters are doing, but you don't know what the scene looks like. You depend greatly on the instruction of the director during the taping to visually set things up in your mind. You go over the script once. You read it again for timing, and then you do it. There's a general read-through for no time whatsoever. Then there's a second read-through for space and timing. Then you record. Half the session is just reading through your lines. Then you mark your part and make a circle around the character you play.

The producer, director, and entire voice cast all participate during the session. They'll give you instructions. The director may say, "Now make it very loud this time, because you're supposed to be over a canyon." Or they might say, "You're over a vat of molten lava, and you're yelling at them."

They explain exactly what the cartoon is about. Sometimes the director will go through the script using storyboards—a series of rudimentary drawings that illustrate what the entire week's episode or story is about—but not always. By the same token, you still are using your own imagination. One person is telling you what's up there (supposedly) on the screen, and you're analyzing what they just said, and it's up to you to deliver on your mark.

Basically, doing cartoon voice-overs is almost the same as acting in a film or television show. The only difference is that all the action is in the voice. If you're in a movie and are fighting with someone who has a stuntman, the voice is laid in later. You go back into the studio for postproduction. They never use the real sound from the filming.

When working in animated cartoons, leaving a lasting impression on the people you work for is very important. Here I'm with Joe Barbera during postproduction of "Space Ghost and Dino Boy," another popular Hanna-Barbera series I did, in which I played the superhero. The series has been running since 1966.

I think anybody who has been an actor can get some fun out of cartoons. They don't have the time allotted in doing a scene in a motion picture because, in a film, you can take as much time as you want. A line that might take one minute to do in a movie would have to be done in a cartoon in maybe five and a half seconds. Of course, in animated cartoons, they don't give you long lines, for that reason. They want the action to move.

Recording sessions usually last no more than a few hours, but sometimes, depending on the producer (and the budget), you may be required to record episodes back-to-back on the same day. When I did my first superhero cartoon series, "Roger Ramjet," we would record about twenty episodes at a session. We'd go in at seven at night and finish at three in the morning. Obviously, this isn't always the case, but having an emergency supply of No Doz or a sharp stick on the boomer really helps.

Proper Etiquette

When working on your first animated cartoon, besides being able to do great cartoon characterizations, following proper studio etiquette at all times is very important. Here are three rules that come to mind.

Leave a Lasting Impression

After getting that first cartoon voice-over job, you want to leave a lasting impression. You hope that doing great work will cause producers to remember you and call you back.

The first time I ever worked for Walt Disney was in 1961. I was hired to do a re-narration of Jerry Colonna's "Casey at the Bat" and also a Goofy cartoon. I didn't know it at the time, but Walt Disney was going to direct the session. I had interviewed him earlier for the Hollywood Museum that was to be constructed, but I didn't know him well.

Before Walt came into the recording studio, one of the engineers said, "Clean up these papers. Mr. Disney is coming." They wanted the recording studio spotless. The doors to the studio were about six inches thick, for providing the acoustics. They had built the recording studio during World War II so it could also double as a hospital if needed in Burbank in a time of war. Anyway, as I was leaning against the door, an engineer on the other side didn't see me and slammed my hand in the door and broke my thumb, and I was bleeding. This all happened just before Mr. Disney said, "Hi, Gary, remember me? I'm Walt Disney."

I said, "Well, of course, Mr. Disney. You'll have to excuse me, but I'm bleeding to death on your carpet."

At that point, he said, "You are, aren't you?" He got on the phone, and a nurse was there in minutes. She put a splint on my thumb, and I was in terrible agony as I narrated Goofy ("Well, Goofy will be out fishing today . . . ") and announced "Casey at the Bat."

I obviously did something right. Since then, I've done hundreds of things for Disney. I was the voice of "The Wonderful World of Disney" for seven years, recorded narratives for Walt Disney World in Orlando and Disneyland, and have done many cartoons, including the announcer on the "Buzz Lightyear" TV series. I'm not saying you should split open your thumb in order to make an impression, but how well you handle yourself in emergencies might leave you in good standing after a long day's work.

Get Along with Others

Obviously, when a bunch of talented people—producers, casting directors, and voice artists—are together in one room, you should try to get along with your peers, even when you don't see eye to eye . . . especially with the director.

At Joe Barbera's ninety-second birthday party at the Warner Brothers Animation Building in Sherman Oaks, hundreds of friends gathered to pay homage to the cartoon legend. When I spoke, I recalled an incident with Joe and Howie Morris of "The Sid Caesar Show." Howie is not only a great cartoon voice and actor but a fine director as well.

Some years ago, Howie and Joe were arguing over a scene in a Hanna-Barbera cartoon, and Howie threw up his hands and yelled, "That's it, I'm leaving. Go screw yourself!" to Joe.

Howie left. For about a year, he did not work there. Then, one day, he was called in to do a cartoon voice. Sheepishly, Howie walked down the long hallway to the recording studio. At that point, Joe Barbera came out of his office and hugged him.

"Howie, how are you?" Joe asked.

Howie mumbled, "I didn't think you'd let me work here again after what I said to you."

Joe smiled and said, "What did you say?"

Howie said, "I told you to go screw yourself."

Joe paused and said, "I took your advice!"

No Jaw Dropping Allowed

Becoming a cartoon voice artist will give you the opportunity to work with many famous people throughout your career. This is certainly no reason for jaw dropping. Treat them as you would any friend . . . and pick up the check and curtsy.

One day, I was at the L.A. Studios to record, and Mel Gibson and I entered the building at the same time. I was doing the announcing for "Bobby's World" with Howie Mandel. I said to him, "You're a movie star. What are you doing over here?"

Mel said, "Well, I'm doing the voice of a chicken." He was working on the animated feature *Chicken Run*. I was doing the voice of a Ham Sandwich for "Bobby's World." As the great *Variety* columnist Army Archerd said, "Only in Hollywood!"

Miracles Do Happen—Even in Cartoons

I've witnessed many incredible things during my career, but none has inspired me more than one remarkable story of overcoming adversity that shows miracles do happen—even in animated cartoons.

In 1962, during the height of TV's first long-running prime-time animated series, "The Flintstones" (in which my friend Mel Blanc was the voice of Barney Rubble), Mel was in a terrible car accident in an area known as Dead Man's Curve on Sunset Boulevard. The year before his accident, six people had died on the same zigzag street with the sharp back-and-forth turns. He saw headlights coming toward him, and an auto swerved across the line and slammed into him head-on. Nearly every bone in his body was smashed from this near-fatal traffic accident, and he was in a coma for three weeks.

Miraculously, on February 14, Mel came out of the coma, and fortunately, his famous voice was still fine. He was in a full-body cast for some seven months, but thanks to his wonderful perseverance and friends and family, he was able to continue working from his bedroom. Producer Joe Barbera and the super cast of "The Flintstones" came in and recorded forty animated cartoons with him. Alan Dinehart directed the shows, cuing the cast from one side of the bedroom. Alan Reed (Fred Flintstone) was there. Jean VanderPyl (Wilma) was alongside, and Bea Benaderet (Betty Rubble) stood on the tanglement of wires while microphone and recording nerf piled up on the floor. ABC Television also recorded new voice-over material for "The Bugs Bunny Show" from the same sleeping room. Friz Freleng and Chuck Jones worked together on the direction of those cartoons. Mel's devoted son, Noel, held the script and flipped the pages while the engineer held the mike to Mel's mouth. (Then, to make it even, Mel held the engineer to Mike's mouth.)

You Be the Character

You've always thought you had the right voice to do cartoons. Well, here's your chance to star in my new "reality" cartoon series, "You Be the Character." I call it a virtual cartoon series in print, since there is no sound studio, no producer, and, sorry, no budget. I can't really pay you, but look on the bright side—now you can carve out a whole career for yourself as cartoon voice artist, thanks to yours truly.

Here's how the series works. It's very simple—so simple you don't need to read the manual or dress up in a goofy costume with freckles painted all over your face. No, instead, all it takes is a little imagination, a little conviction on your part, and the sound of your voice. Ready to play along? Good. Position yourself in front of a tape recorder—and, of course, a microphone. Clean your heads—on the tape recorder—so your tape doesn't stick. A little alcohol and cotton swab will do the trick. Now you're all set.

For our first round, you get to play the narrator for "Eek the Cat!" Yes, the same narration that I did in so many households across America. Your job is to be dramatic. After all, that's what a narrator does: draws people into the action. Nervous? Oh, don't be; this is only a book, and this *isn't* the real series. Just play along and have fun. Maybe do a few practice readings. That should help. Follow the script and read along. Actually, don't just read the part, play the part. Pretend Savage Steve Holland and Bill Kopp are directing you. Remember, this is your job in a major cartoon series.

In doing your practice readings, get yourself into the mood. Also, picture the scene, and imagine the setting and the place in time in which the story is taking place. Usually, the narrative cues preceding the dialogue tell you this, as in the following sample script, courtesy of the Nelvana Company:

EEK-MEN

We pan across the majestic mountain range far above the sparkling city of Metropolis.

GARY OWENS

Far above the beautiful city of Metropolis on a secluded mountaintop lies the home of the city's favorite fighter of crime and protector of good . . . SUPERPERSONMAN!

The camera trucks in toward a glass dome on the top of one of the mountains. It looks ridiculous and somewhat like a gumball machine.

GARY OWENS

Deep within the Bunker of Goodness, Superpersonman is getting an important message from his all-seeing "Info-orbital-penelope-spheres," the sacred and mysterious glass ball of wisdom and knowledge given to Superpersonman by his grandfather, who had it handed down to him by his own grandfather, who in turn received the sacred orb from his sister's aunt's chiropractor, who got it from her uncle Ted, who misplaced it for a number of weeks.

Gasp! Sorry. I tried holding my breath and reading at the same time and found you can't do both. Anyway, now that you've practiced, you're ready for the next big step: pushing the Play button on your tape recorder.

Remember, follow the script and read along. Don't just read the part, play the part of a big-voiced narrator. That's it! You're sounding better already. Now try it one more time to really get the hang of it. You want to make it to our final bonus round. Again, once more. That's better. Perfect! Do as many takes as you need. Remember, you're in show biz now.

Gosharooties! My producer tells me we have run out of time and there's only time for one more round on the show before pronouncing our winner. (So many commercials, so little time.)

This time you're going to get to play a superhero. That's right—save the world, and everybody's happy. Essentially, as a superhero, you'll be doing the same voice as a narrator but as someone with "superpowers." So be a superbeing with a supervoice. Not all whiny. Super!

Let me hear it: "Super!"

I think you've got it.

Setting the scene once again, you're playing the character Captain Squash, from the hit cartoon series "Bobby's World" with Howie Mandel. No, Howie's not here. He's vacationing in the Swiss Alps with a bunch of Eskimos, who are busy frying cube steaks for breakfast. However, he tells me he sends his best, and for you to play along anyway.

In this story, as Captain Squash, you're out to save Bobby's sister, Kelly, who's been abducted by a big bad Wolf. Look, I don't write the scripts (that's the job of talented Jim Fisher and Jim Stahl, great funny guys from "Second City"); I only read them.

Seriously, now do a few practice readings as you did before, when you played the narrator. For this particular reading, find someone to do the voices of Bobby and the Wolf. Read the narrative cues beforehand, and imagine now that you are the great and powerful Captain Squash, who rids the world of evil menaces. (Gary Conrad is producing the animation on today's episode.) Action!

BOBBY'S WORLD

EXT. A CABIN IN THE WOODS—PANNING

Bobby and CAPTAIN SQUASH rush up to the cabin and, in true superhero fashion, kick the door open. (NOTE: The door is a two-sectioned Dutch door, but it swings open like a one-piece door for now.)

BOBBY'S POV—KELLY AND THE WOLF—PANNING

The wolf is chasing a terrified Kelly. (NOTE: The Wolf looks and sounds like Freddy Krueger.)

ON BOBBY

                    BOBBY

You leave my sister alone.

ON THE WOLF

Whirling around to Bobby, growling.

ANGLE ON SQUASH AND BOBBY

            CAPTAIN SQUASH

Uh-oh.

(To Wolf) Give me a minute here, would you, ma'am?

Captain Squash leads Bobby off to the side.

                    BOBBY

But Captain Squash, we have to save Kelly.

            CAPTAIN SQUASH

I have a bad feeling about this, Bobby. Let me consult the Captain
Squash Manual.

He opens the manual and pages through.

            CAPTAIN SQUASH

Let's see. Things Captain Squash likes to wear. No. Things
Captain Squash likes to eat. No. Ah, here it is. Things Captain
Squash is afraid of: Monsters. No problem. . . . Ghosts. A little
nervous about . . . Wolves. . . . (Really scared!)

And that's a wrap!

As you can see, doing animated cartoon voices can be a great profession as well as a whole lot of fun; it's like being in a high school play with a bunch of your friends and classmates. At least the painting of the sets is not up to you but handled by the many wonderfully gifted animators who are well paid to do what they do best.

In case you are a beginner and think you'll never have an opportunity, here's a wonderful success story to inspire you: When Bob Bergen was eight years old, the one thing in life he aspired to be was the voice of Porky Pig. After the death of Mel Blanc, Warner Brothers auditioned hundreds of voices, and Bob was chosen—a lifelong dream come true!

What's that? You're excited. I'm happy for you. Oh, the next chapter? No, you didn't think the book ended here. I have much more to tell. Sharing time isn't over. Just flip the page, and G.O. will show you everything there is about emceeing and public speaking—and making money doing it, too.

10

Have Voice, Will Travel

Emceeing and Speaking in Public

WORKING AS A master of ceremonies or public speaker can be one of the most glamorous jobs, takes considerable energy and preparation, and is well paid. Whether you're attending a bar mitzvah, hosting a testimonial dinner, or speaking at the local Save the Beaver Club, using your voice in this way not only gives you the opportunity to use your talent but also adds another dimension to your career as a voice professional.

I have done thousands of speaking engagements over the years, either emceeing a local event or appearing as a keynote speaker at a major convention. No matter what the case, doing this kind of work has proven very worthwhile.

Using my stage voice as emcee for concerts, I have been fortunate to work with some of the biggest stars in the world, including such greats as Tony Bennett; Paul and Linda McCartney; the Big Bopper; Sir Elton John; Lenny Bruce; Steve and Eydie Gorme; the Carpenters; Judy Garland; Henry Mancini; Bob Hope; Natalie Cole; Nat King Cole; the Kingston Trio; Peggy Lee; Sir Rod Stewart; Madonna; Liza Minnelli; Peter, Paul and Mary; the Dwarves; Cheech and Chong; Elvis Presley;

Emceeing an event is different from public speaking. Your role is to officiate over the proceedings, as I did here for the ceremony renaming Catalina Street as Bob Hope Drive. Pictured (left to right) are yours truly, the late Brandon Tartikoff, then head of NBC's entertainment division, Dolores Hope, and the legendary Bob Hope.

Johnny Mathis; Frank Sinatra Sr. and Jr.; Julie Andrews; Barbra Streisand; and Andy Williams, to name a few.

Not only have I worked with some very famous people, but I also have emceed everything you can possibly imagine, including major Hollywood movie premieres, Hollywood Walk of Fame star induction ceremonies, groundbreakings, dedications, and many other major Hollywood events.

One of my big thrills was emceeing the changing of Catalina Street in Burbank to Bob Hope Drive next to the NBC Studios. I have guest-starred on a number of Bob's television specials and emceed many concerts with Rapid Robert. I've known Bob and Dolores Hope for more than forty years. The street renaming was a wonderful honor. The late Brandon Tartikoff, then head of NBC's entertainment division, was there, and the quips on Bob's great career were zooming around the stage. I mentioned that the NBC commissary had a luncheon special that day, "a scoop of mashed potatoes in the shape of Bob's nose."

For many years, I've also emceed the L.A. Press Club's Headliners of the Year Awards honoring the likes of Bob Barker, Neil Simon, Marcia Clark, Marsha Mason, Christopher Darden, Ralph Edwards, and Martin Landau. The city of Los Angeles gave Marcia Clark a $14,300 bonus for her work on the O. J. Simpson trial, which was about as much as Johnny Cochran spent on dry-cleaning his suits!

For thirty years, I did the introductions and play-by-play at Dodger Stadium in Los Angeles for the annual All-Star Celebrity Baseball Game, which was played before the regular Dodgers game. Major Hollywood stars would come out to play or coach. Some of those partaking of the great national pastime were Dean Martin, John Beradino, Robert Conrad, Ted Knight, Ross Martin, Bob Newhart, Carl Reiner, Rob Reiner, Walter Matthau, Jack Lemmon, Telly Savalas, Billy Barty, Kareem Abdul Jabbar, Mark Harmon, Lou Ferrigno, Frank Sinatra, Danny Kaye, Billy Crystal, Greg Morris, Lou Rawls, Elliot Gould, Robin Williams, Ed Asner, Jonathan Winters, and Jon Lovitz.

Of the Hollywood starlets who partook in the event, most were coaches and bat girls, including Elaine Boozler, Pamela Anderson, Annette Funicello, Morgan Fairchild, Loretta Swit, Morgana the Kissing Bandit, Linda Blair, and Heather Locklear.

Whether you are emceeing a local parade, supermarket opening, or church social or speaking on a topic of great interest to a local club, group, or organization, you can carve out a nice niche for yourself in either profession, so long as you know what you are doing.

Opportunities for Speakers

Various organizations are always looking for speakers to address their monthly meetings, conventions, or other events and often will pay from small to outrageous fees for your services. Oftentimes many of these same groups may be seeking someone to serve as a master of ceremonies of a soiree! No matter which avenue you take, before you enter this lion's den, it helps to have a plan of action for adequately developing your speaking and presentation skills.

Emceeing an event involves a different style than public speaking. An emcee is an entertainer whose role is to officiate, if you will, over the proceedings, be they testimonial dinners or star-studded events; to introduce important guests; to make funny little remarks during segues to keep the audience involved; and generally to keep the proceedings running perfectly. Public speakers at times can be entertaining, even humorous, but their primary purpose is to inform their audience on the topic for which they have been invited to speak. In this case, they deliver a prepared speech, usually on a topic of their choosing.

You can avoid many problems if you work out the kinks in your presentation—and in your back—beforehand. Major drawbacks that undermine people's presentations usually occur because presenters have not properly prepared, rehearsed their material, or honed their craft well enough to have the confidence to do what they have been paid to do.

At some point in time, you may be called upon to emcee or do some public speaking or want to pursue either of these more aggressively as another means to an end. Whether an engagement is your first experience or your thousandth, the way you present yourself can mean the difference between your audience responding to you or having yourself escorted to the nearest exit, where your presentation on "Investing in Wheat Germ" may be better received.

Conquer Your Fear

The first and most important step to becoming a successful emcee or public speaker is overcoming your fear of speaking in front of others. Conquering your nervousness is crucial to commanding your audience's attention. If you are a Naturally Nervous Nellie, there's a simple five-part cure for your fear:

1. **Imagine you are perfect.** Whether or not this is your first job as emcee or public speaker, mistakes will happen. But this doesn't mean you are less than perfect—even if your cummerbund is on backward or falls off on the stage, as mine once did, at the Forum in Los Angeles.

2. **Think happy thoughts.** Keeping the right frame of mind at all times—thinking happy thoughts—will help you overcome any fear, and your uneasiness will surely fade . . . even if people are laughing at the wrong places.

3. **Be positive.** Stop worrying, and enjoy yourself. You have something important to do or something important to say, and others want to hear it. This is the moment you have been waiting for!

4. **Forget your past.** Those who emcee or do public speaking all have had some humiliating incident happen to them at one time or another, yet they come back for more. Pick yourself up. Brush yourself off. You know the song.

5. **Look your best.** It's important not only to act but also to dress the part. Work on your appearance so you look and feel your best, or people will notice.

In 1983, when I sponsored the drive to get the Three Stooges their star (working with Jeff and Greg Lenburg, who were instrumental in the process), Milton Berle was on hand at the unveiling and said one of the best quips about me. I wore a pin-striped suit that day and looked more like a mobster than a master of ceremonies. Speaking before five thousand people who had gathered for the occasion (many had been there since 7:00 A.M.), Milton, who never missed a beat, said, "This occasion is both fitting and proper, which is more than I can say about Gary Owens's suit!"

One final point: When emceeing or doing public speaking, just remember that your audience truly wants you to succeed. Most would never do what you do and risk embarrassment, humiliation, or failure, but they admire you for having the courage to get up and entertain them or

When I emceed the Hollywood Walk of Fame ceremony for the Three Stooges, Milton Berle reminded me always to look my best. He said, "This occasion is both fitting and proper, which is more than I can say about Gary Owens's suit!"

speak your mind and are generally on your side—even if many people have shifted to the other side of the room.

Speaking Effectively

Speaking well, and not as if your mouth is full of cotton or you're still under general anesthesia after having three teeth pulled by your dentist, will make a gigantic difference. To make a positive impression on your audience and those paying your fee, follow these suggestions:

1. **Attitude.** Have a good attitude about where you'll be speaking and to whom. Nothing can more seriously undermine your success than

having the wrong attitude and letting others see it. As my friend Phyllis Diller once said, "A smile is the curve that sets everything straight." So straighten out that crooked smile, stranger. Get up there and shine.

2. Preparation. Organize your presentation. Know what you want to say and when. This will help to eliminate any *umms* in your speech pattern. Umm, know what I mean?

3. Delivery. Don't hurry your speech as though you're racing in the Indy 500 and are trying to set a new world speed record. Be comfortable, visualize yourself being successful as you speak, and control the rate of your speech (faster or slower) to keep your audience alert . . . and awake!

4. Interaction. Get the audience involved so they're relaxed and receptive to your presentation. Be courteous and thoughtful when interacting with others.

Know Your Audience

An important rule of emceeing or speaking in public is that you should know your audience. Once you are booked for an engagement, find out something outstanding or notable about them in advance. This will help you make your speech more timely and relevant. It may also make you feel more comfortable and help you to develop your speech, even if it's a speech you've given to another group—perhaps tweaking it just a bit so you don't alienate your audience.

If I have found anything to be true about emceeing or public speaking, it's that all audiences are different and none are perfect. So don't go into this thinking you can control their behavior. If someone is restless or fidgety, it may have nothing to do with you!

Many public speakers fail to do this, so they lose their audience. The first signs of losing an audience are:

1. You're not the only person talking.
2. They leave early . . . five minutes before you start.

Speaking well and making a positive impression on your audience go hand in hand. Here, Gene Hackman admires my invisible hand puppet at the world premiere of *Superman*.

3. The fried chicken sale in the parking lot has a much longer line.

4. People suddenly get up to dance—and without music.

5. The janitors start putting away the folding chairs, and everyone in attendance starts helping them, and you're still speaking.

6. The snoring is so loud in the room that you can't even hear yourself speak.

7. The pizza delivery guy comes back too many times, and you didn't place an order.

8. The Fat Lady sings.

9. A large group is protesting outside—against you!

10. The Fat Lady sings an encore.
11. Everyone asks for a refund.

Project Style and Substance

As an emcee or public speaker, you should have some idea beforehand of the type of image you want to project in your presentation and to your audience. Along with substance to your speech or material, the key is developing a speaking style that audiences will receive and remember. The style of a successful public speaker has the following important elements:

1. **Be genuine.** Nothing will impress an audience more than if you come across as genuine. So will being a big tipper!
2. **Be sincere.** Being sincere with your audience can have the same effect.
3. **Be humble.** Being humble in front of others will make you more credible, more believable, and more respected. Your audience will connect with you more easily if you become one of them—unless they belong to some strange cult.

Relax

To help put yourself at ease, no matter when and where you will be emceeing or speaking, arrive early at the venue to familiarize yourself with your surroundings. Casually circulate and introduce yourself to the organizers, staff, and people who arrived early themselves to hear your presentation. Always smile, act friendly, and be confident.

Take time to relax physically and mentally while waiting for your turn. Many famous entertainers I have known through the years do little things to keep themselves relaxed: take a deep breath, meditate, play a favorite song in their mind, think of the people they love or something outstanding they did recently. This way, you won't keep thinking about the fact you'll have to get up on stage soon.

When your name is called, walk as you normally do up to the podium. Confidently position yourself in front of the microphone, smile, look at all the people around you, and jump into your speech—not off the stage.

Ten Commandments of Emceeing and Public Speaking

To improve your emceeing and speaking skills and deliver better presentations—and thus better results—consider these simple rules, which I call my Ten Commandments of Emceeing and Public Speaking:

1. **Thou shalt know thy material.** Nothing can be more embarrassing than not knowing your material when speaking or entertaining an audience. Don't try to wing it, or you'll break into a cold sweat for sure. Know your material. Take time to prepare and rehearse your speech thoroughly so you look and act professional when you speak. This will help you avoid a multitude of problems that could arise.

2. **Thou shalt K.I.S.S. (keep it simple, stupid).** Speak to your audience in a language they understand. The truth is, the best emcees or public speakers usually use a simple approach. They get their ideas across in a memorable way and communicate simply to their audience without getting too detailed or intricate. And limit your hand puppet presentations, please. You can communicate your ideas as simply as possible if you first think through the points you want to make and then write your speech around them.

3. **Thou shalt speak naturally.** Be yourself and act naturally when you speak. Don't try to be something or someone you're not. Imitating other great speakers or great masters of ceremonies won't help you. Just talk the way you would normally. Be that charismatic, wonderful person you always have been with your friends, or at parties, or at the prom, even if you did spit tobacco on your date's dress.

4. **Thou shalt not overspeak.** Don't cram too much material into your presentation, call attention to every slide or visual aid you're show-

When emceeing or speaking in public, always be yourself. Here I am presenting the prestigious Lifetime Achievement Award to Sammy Davis Jr. from the important Hollywood Press Club. I told Sammy I brought contact raisins for the Gingerbread Man.

ing, and become so detail oriented that someone has to buy Cliff Notes to understand what you are saying (or to understand your jokes!).

5. Thou shalt be passionate . . . about thy material. Ah, I got your attention with that one. Let your passion flow from within you. Your audience will be more responsive if you are passionate about your material. You can achieve this through the inflection of your voice and by communicating your ideas enthusiastically. This will make your audience excited about your presentation.

6. Thou shalt covet thine audience. Looking at only one person in the audience will lose your audience right away. They'll feel left out, and you want them all to feel part of your entire presentation and speaking experience, so include them. Make them part of your presentation. The best way to do this is to make eye contact. Look to those on the left side of the room, then those in the middle, then those on the right, and look at different people in different sections to keep everyone enthused and interested.

7. Thou shalt watch thy gestures. Perhaps you grew up in an Italian or Greek household, and wildly gesturing with your hands is how you get your point across. When you are emceeing or speaking in public, hand gestures can be a useful tool, but when they are overused, all that your audience notices is your frenetic hand gestures, and no one is paying attention to what you are saying. Pointing your finger and pounding your fist on the podium are definite no-nos. If you are unable to control yourself, rest your hands on either side of the podium, or simply fold your hands in front of you or in back of you. Obviously, you should never try to do all three of these at once!

8. Thou shalt not wobble. More than wild hand gestures, nothing will alienate your audience more than rocking back and forth from one foot to the other while you speak. This nasty habit will distract your audience to the point you'll make some drowsy—and others eager to nail down your feet.

9. Thou shalt show and not tell. Giving examples and telling stories or a few jokes can enliven your presentation. Rambling on endlessly can cause serious trouble—especially if the audience thinks you missed your latest therapy session. Keep your presentation balanced, and paint a vivid picture that everyone can enjoy.

10. Thou shalt not overstay. Just because everyone is having a good time and your speech is going along swimmingly is no reason to stay longer than you intended. Short and sweet and to the point will leave a lasting impression on your audience. They will be more enthusiastic about having you back in the future than if you droned on for another half hour because they requested it. "Leave 'em wanting," I always say.

Tips and Techniques for Emceeing

Other techniques are also involved in becoming a successful emcee. Johnny Grant is one of the top emcees in the United States and around the world and has been my pal for many years. He performed with Bob Hope for decades, entertaining our troops for the legendary USO. As Hollywood's honorary mayor, he has emceed every star ceremony for the Hollywood Walk of Fame. I asked Johnny for his tips on becoming a successful emcee. He offered the following:

- An emcee should generate excitement.

- Provide whoever will be introducing you as the emcee with any information and credits that you will need to reference as a lead-in to material you'll be using during the course of the event.

- Arrive at the event early, giving yourself time to gather extraneous and topical information. Always have something prepared to use as filler, should there be an emergency and the program is stalled.

- Before the event, say hello to the people you're to introduce. Ask them if there are any special credits they want mentioned. And remember that people are very proud of their names and the way they are pronounced. If you have any doubt about pronunciation, be sure to check with the person being introduced or the program chairman.

- Don't rely on your memory. Use notes.

- The quality of your introduction for civic and public officials and corporate types can build a lot of political currency and goodwill—not only for you but also for the organization you're supporting by emceeing the event.

- Understand that many corporate CEOs and politicians have egos comparable to that of any entertainment celebrity. In their minds, they *are* stars and seek that kind of treatment.

- If you're going to use humor, it's always safer to make sure it's family style. Make yourself comfortable with your comedy material before you attempt to deliver it to an audience.

- Don't introduce people with "roast" type jokes unless the event has been billed as that kind of an occasion. Never take a chance on offending the audience or program participants.

- An emcee should know how to discreetly "use the hook" when a speaker is long-winded. Each person has a unique style of doing this, and a good emcee will develop one that fits his or her persona. You should have a prepared routine for this situation.

Developing Your Speech

Always try to be original when giving speeches. Whatever speech you give really should reflect your personality and give your audience something of value. Whenever I have been asked to write a speech for a special event or occasion, I follow five basic principles:

1. **Give them something to remember.** It's important to give your audience three essential messages, three things they are likely to remember. The best way to do this is to think of what you would want to say if you had only ten seconds to say it.

2. **Stick to short sentences.** Don't get too wordy or long-winded, and write your speech as if you are talking to a friend.

3. **Keep your speech upbeat.** When people come to hear you speak, they usually want to walk away feeling happy. Use a more positive approach to getting your message across so your speech will be well received.

4. Use humor when appropriate. As the great Martin Luther King Jr. once said, "Humor is a divine quality, and God has the greatest sense of all. He must have, otherwise he wouldn't have made so many politicians." Humor can be a useful element to make your speech more memorable. Many famous politicians have hired gag writers over the years to punch up their talks, and many more could have benefited from hiring one! For example, when Richard Nixon was president, he hired Paul Keyes, head writer for "Laugh-In." When John Lindsey was mayor of New York, he hired Woody Allen, and Pat Buttram wrote gags for Ronald Reagan.

Remember, any humor or jokes should flow naturally in your speech and not be forced. Avoid the "three men going into a bar" jokes, especially if you don't know the punch line. Also avoid using any humor that may be offensive. You don't want to risk offending someone!

5. Add famous quotations. Nothing can spice up a dull speech better than a smattering of famous quotes that people can identify with. The quotes can be humorous or thought provoking, and you should take the time to carefully select the quote that's most appropriate to the event you're hosting. You can find quotes such as these at any local public library or by checking out various websites on the Internet (enter "famous quotes" in your search engine).

Sample Speeches

Recently, I was asked to address the National Collegiate Broadcasters convention in Los Angeles. As a keynote speaker at this event, I developed a speech that was aimed at the youngest, brightest minds in broadcasting and would not only elevate them but also entertain them. The following is what I wrote:

> *Thank you for asking me to be your keynote speaker here today. I hope you all continue in the broadcasting business and become great successes.*
>
> *I must warn you, however, that the average stay for a disc jockey at any one station in the U.S. is a year and a half. And*

let me enumerate with casual, somber rapidity, the occupational hazards of being an on-the-air personality. Excessive smoking, dipsomania, hemorrhoids, impotence, overreliance on uppers, dyspepsia, and chronic anxiety—and those are just the good things!

I've been in this bizarre business since I was sixteen (I'm now eighteen) and have seen the metamorphoses of the last twenty years. Someone, I believe it was the famous philosopher Bo Diddley, once said, "The audience will forgive you for being wrong and exciting but never for being right and dull."

One of the broadcasters here today asked, "Garish, what does an on-the-air personality actually do in a major-market station?" ("Garish" was a regular nickname for me—by other members of my radio show!) Well, of course, most of the time you're filling out the log and preparing what you're going to back announce. But the G.O. Foundation surveyed seven thousand DJs around the nation, and we found that 51 percent of the DJs tie a teabag to their zippers and they try to hypnotize dwarf record promoters!

Thirty-seven percent see how many No. 2 pencils will fit in their nose.

Ten percent shove the headphone cord into their pants and listen to their underwear. . . .

Certainly, my speech to this fine young group was much longer than this, but you get the picture. You want to aim your speech at the audience to whom you are speaking and in a way that becomes engaging. That's all there is to it. Of course, when finishing your speech, be sure to thank your audience again for having you.

When emceeing an event, it's important to write a speech that is appropriate for the occasion. Emceeing is like performing, and it helps to have good material at these functions to make them memorable for everyone involved. I usually write material that reflects my offbeat personality and sense of humor. Perhaps joining a social club where you get an opportunity to practice speaking would be wise.

Over the years, I emceed several events honoring my friend the late great comedian Steve Allen. At one such dinner, I wrote the following to read as the emcee:

> *I first met Steve Allen in 1959 in San Francisco. He was always very kind to me. We immediately became pun pals. A mutual friend, Niles Lishness (yes, there really is a Niles Lishness), invited me to the Fairmont Hotel, and in my shy, midwestern way, I took my hat in my hands and meandered up to Steve's suite, where he was writing a speech to be delivered to a group of California literary mavens.*
>
> *At his desk, he also wrote two new songs that afternoon. As you know, Steve has written over seven thousand songs. Whatever happened to him, he wrote a song about it. One of his hits was "I Passed a Kidney Stone"!*
>
> *Steve was there when George Greeley and I were recording his composition "What Is a Freem?" George played his famous piano, and I narrated. It came out on Warner Brothers Records.*

Another time, I emceed a star-studded salute to Loretta Young for the Variety Club International when it honored her with its prestigious Humanitarian Award. Naturally, to emcee this important event, I adapted my speech to fit the occasion and the personality they were honoring:

> *It's my pleasure to proudly present one of the greatest ladies of movies and television.*
>
> *She began in film at the age of four and has starred in close to a hundred big-screen features, winning an Oscar for* The Farmer's Daughter *and two Emmys for Best Actress in a Continuing Series.*
>
> *During those wonderful days, she was famous also for her swear box she kept on the set of her TV show. (Tonight, I'm sure that everyone is thankful the talented George Carlin is not emceeing with his "Seven Famous Words.")*

Rising to the Occasion

Just because your material is well rehearsed and perfectly scripted doesn't mean you shouldn't prepared for the unexpected. By this, I mean being able to change your material midstream and handle any disruptions.

One year, when I was the master of ceremonies at the National Association of Broadcasters (NAB) convention, I had to put this plan into motion. I had done thirty minutes of shtick before introducing Joan Rivers. I went through my introduction. "Ladies and gentlemen, the funniest lady in America and the world, Joan Rivers." But Joan didn't come out. There was no Joan.

I made up something. "Joan's probably knitting an afghan right now for Eddie Fritts," head of the NAB. Still Joan didn't appear.

Finally, somebody offstage came over and said, "She's upstairs. She doesn't want people from the *Los Angeles Times* here because they put her down in a critique, and she won't come down unless they leave."

I said, "Now's a wonderful time to tell us."

So I had to fill for another forty minutes. I went out into the audience and ad-libbed. I went up to a well-dressed man in a black tuxedo and said, "Tell me a little bit about yourself."

The man didn't say anything. So I kept prodding him. "You never poisoned your wife, I guess."

The man reluctantly spoke up. "Well, once."

I also chatted with the always fun V.P. of the NAB—John David—who described how when starting in the biz as a DJ in Oklahoma he would interview farm animals and fence posts.

I kept things moving until finally Joan came out—and the audience didn't seem to mind, so long as they were still entertained. In fact, I got a standing ovation!

Of course, when emceeing, speaking in public, or being a participant at these functions, you can't control everything.

Knowing When You Have Succeeded

How do you know if you have succeeded? At what point do you know if your speech or performance was well received and the people who booked you were pleased? Obviously, so long as none of the local villagers stormed the place, carrying torches and pickaxes, then it's safe to say you did well. Of course, this isn't the only way to determine if you were well liked. You know your speech was successful if:

- People walk away with something of value.

- They walk away feeling better about themselves.

- They leave feeling better about something they have to do that will transform their lives.

- They leave feeling happy or entertained.

- They consider their time with you worthwhile.

As you can see, emceeing and speaking in public aren't as difficult as they sound. In fact, this career choice can be fun, exciting, and prosperous. Many entertainers earn more than $50,000 per speech.

Miscellany — or, "That's All, Folks!"

WHEN LAUNCHING YOUR career as a famous voice artist, don't forget miscellany. There are a variety of sundry ways you can sell and market your voice besides the avenues we've already discussed. Your options include narrating audiobooks, films, and videos and providing voices for toys and games.

Opportunities for Narrators

Narrators are the unsung heroes of the voice-over world. They are heard on thousands of documentaries, television movies, feature films, industrial films, audiobooks, instructional videos, CDs, and DVDs. This is another area that offers untold possibilities for you to use your voice. Narration is a form of creativity that has transcended time and technology.

I have had the great pleasure of working in all of these fields. I have provided narration for more than twenty-five audiobooks, including such titles as *The Cosby Wit: His Life and Humor*; *Legends, Lies & Cherished*

Myths; The Wit and Wisdom of Dan Quayle; and *The Final Generation*. I've done more than thirty videos and DVDs. Among them have been retrospectives, instructional videos, and documentaries. I've done my share of film and television narration as well. I've lent my voice to many major motion picture and television productions, feature films, and hundreds of industrial films over the years. In addition, I've dabbled in narrating computer games, and I've voiced for several hundred toys, including the vocalization of the Pink Panther doll for Mattel.

Voice artists enjoy great careers as narrators. Some are actors involved in second or third careers. Others are actors who make a living on Broadway (most Broadway shows don't last that long) and on off-Broadway (they last even less). It's a great way to supplement their income. Narrators demonstrate a special or unique quality in their voice that makes them ideally suited for the profession.

Many narrators are former newscasters, mainly because of the nature of their voice. For example, the man who narrated the "NFL Football Films of the Week" for twenty years was John Secondary. He was once a newscaster in Philadelphia. Alexander Scourby, a fine actor, became one of the top narrators for television shows and films. So did the legendary Orson Welles.

Financial rewards can be great for a narrator, which is why more and more artists are doing this kind of work. One can make thousands of dollars. Bruce Willis reportedly made ten million dollars for doing the voice of a baby in *Look Who's Talking Too* (1990).

Narrating Films

Narration is a wonderful pacesetter and art form, especially in motion pictures. For example, in the movie *To Kill a Mockingbird*, author Harper Lee set the mood and tone for the whole movie through the narration of a woman now grown who goes back to being a little girl, playing marbles and so on. Actress Kim Stanley did the narration. This dramatic technique not only was very effective but also provided a key element for telling the film's story.

Besides narrating major film productions, narrators also play an integral role in the success of movie trailers promoting coming attractions.

Where mere images fail, the narrator's voice comes to the rescue, creating excitement for the film the trailer is promoting. There's a whole business in just doing movie trailers. My chum Don LaFontaine, whose voice is perfect for this type of production, is probably the biggest money earner in the business today, making $3.5 million to $4.5 million a year.

Film narration has its share of benefits, especially if the film you've narrated is recognized in a special way. This can only help your career. In 2002 I provided narration for the short subject *The Tortoise and the Hare*, which premiered at the Egyptian Theater in Hollywood as part of the American Cinematheque's Tribute to Ray Harryhausen. The short film, which was selected for competition at the Sundance Film Festival, just missed being nominated that year for an Oscar for Best Animated Short Subject and won an Anny Award in 2003 as best cartoon at the International Animated Film Society (ASIFA) awards show.

Even working as a narrator has its hazards. William Conrad learned the importance of pacing when he narrated the "Rocky and Bullwinkle" cartoons for Jay Ward. One time, Ward thought Conrad was too slow reading the narration during a taping, so he took a match and lit the end of Conrad's script so he'd read *faster*.

Some jobs you never forget. I used to narrate films for the Orange County Medical Association in the 1960s. One film I narrated was *How to Give an Enema*, teaching young, up-and-coming nurses the technique of inflicting rectal discomfort on millions of men and women. (This was before my days on "Laugh-In.") I've narrated lots of industrial films as a result. Invariably, I have received mail from young nurses saying they couldn't keep a straight face watching the films I narrated ("First swab the area . . ."), although Siskel and Ebert gave it "two thumbs up!"

Narrating TV Programs and Documentaries

There are many wonderful male and female voice artists who every day set the tone for a television show. To be really successful narrating TV programs and documentaries, you need an agent to represent you. Breaking into this end of the business is much like doing commercials or cartoons. You must put your work on CDs or cassettes to submit to an agent. The agent will, in turn, submit your sound to producers and corporations that

Many other fields of interest allow you to use your voice. The possibilities are as varied as narration for film, television, and audiobooks and recordings for toys and games, like this CD-ROM trivia show I did. The game features countless famous television personalities, including James Doohan ("Star Trek"), Marion Ross ("Happy Days"), G.O., Loretta Swit ("M*A*S*H"), Davy Jones ("The Monkees"), and Jaclyn Smith ("Charlie's Angels").

are looking for narrators. Once you get a few jobs under your belt, anything is possible.

Narrating DVDs

DVDs are an example of a burgeoning marketplace where studios are supplementing their disc versions of film classics with supplementary voice tracks and voice narration. These tracks are usually recorded as narration to explain the history and production of a film. On one hand, they provide insights for film fans; on the other, they favor firsthand recollections of the stars and directors.

Narrating Audiobooks

For years, radio dramatizations were commonplace entertainment, and generations grew up listening to actors recreate their favorite characters and stories on the air. Today, radio dramatizations have been replaced by another fast-growing medium: audiobooks.

Audiobooks, many sold under the Books on Tape brand, have become popular sources of literary dramatizations for consumers who have long weekday commutes to work or enjoy listening while driving on a cross-country trip. Most audiobook listeners are "road warriors" who typically travel in a car, van, or truck and enjoy the convenience of listening to a literary experience on tape in the privacy of their vehicle.

Narrators, in this case, act as conduits between an author's words and an unseen audience. The difference between a good audiobook and a bad one is the quality of the reader. The goal of the reader in doing an audiobook is to capture the author's voice accurately and clearly articulate and communicate the complex ideas, situations, characters, and other nuances in this audio adaptation. Most readers today who are hired for audiobook readings display amazing versatility, while others are more limited in scope. Some readers have a natural gift for humor and do only that specific genre, while others do first-rate readings in multiple genres.

The best readers in the business have a loyal following. Some consumers select audiobooks to borrow or purchase on the basis of who is doing the reading. For example, veteran listeners know George Guidall is

Jim Chee of the Tony Hillerman series and that Barbara Rosenblat is the incomparable Amanda Peabody. Often, on the strength of a favorite narrator, people will buy an audiobook because of the enthralling performance of the skilled reader.

Becoming a professional audiobook narrator requires being at the right place at the right time and possessing a certain level of experience in order to get hired. Some audiobook narrators with little experience are hired because publishers believe they have lots of potential and consider the long-term benefit of hiring someone who isn't as costly as a famous personality. Incomes of audiobook readers vary widely, just as they do for authors. Readers typically make from $50 for an hour of studio time to as much as $900 an hour. Publishers hold an annual forum in New York—JAM (Jobs in the Audiobook Market) for publishers and narrators. There, prescreened narrators audition before an audience of audio publishers.

Recording CDs

Providing your vocal talent on CDs can be yet another avenue for your voice. I've recorded more than twenty albums during my career. Some are records featuring funny bits of business, and on others, I provided a supporting voice or served as the narrator. My very first album was *Song Festoons* in 1961, followed by *Put Your Head on My Finger* for MGM Records. Since then I've plied my voice on a host of other recordings, including *The Funny Side of Bonnie and Clyde* (Epic), *The Hexorcist* (ABC/Dunhill), *Sunday Morning with the Comics* (Reprise), *The Age of Television: A Chronicle of the First 25 Years* (Reprise), *W. C. Fields: Greatest Lines from Movies* (Decca/MCA), *The Marx Brothers* (Decca/MCA), and most recently, *Jonathan Winters and Gary Owens: Outpatients* (Laugh.com) and *Jonathan Winters and Gary Owens—Live at the Improv* (Laugh.com).

Dubbing Voices

Voice dubbing is another extension of the voice-over business. This form lends itself to a wide range of purposes. Many times a producer may need

Other opportunities exist outside the usual. My voice and image are now featured on a new slot machine by Bally in Las Vegas along with my pal Bob Eubanks.

to redo a line of dialogue in a film or dub an entire film in English or in a foreign language. This requires someone capable of stepping in to do a particular actor's voice.

Paul Frees is a good example of someone who enjoyed great success in this field. Originally he was a comic named Buddy Green. He was appearing in Chicago, and apparently one of the casting directors watched his act. Paul would always do Humphrey Bogart, Orson Welles, and Clark Gable in his routine. Bogart liked to drink and disappear when doing a movie so producers couldn't find him to do postproduction, which is when actors are brought back to dub in lines of dialogue. Orson Welles used to disappear as well. He'd fly to Switzerland so the studio couldn't find him. Paul dubbed their voices for scenes in some of their movies, and he made a very good living doing that.

Incidentally, besides being known as the voice of Scrooge McDuck, Paul was the voice of 80 percent of all the rides at Disneyland. For many years, I've been the voice of the Wonderful World of Motion at Disney's EPCOT in Florida, and I'm the narrator for the Hollywood Ride at Disneyland's California Adventure theme park. This just goes to show that for every disembodied voice you hear, there's a person somewhere who was paid to provide it.

Voicing Specialty Products

Other opportunities exist to broaden your creative horizons, not to mention your pocketbook. Products that use voice recordings include voice-messaging systems, toys, and computer and video games.

Voice Messaging

Voice messaging is the rage. It's everywhere—on home answering machines, on computers, and on cell phones. Not all the voices you hear are computer generated; many are performed by experienced voice professionals. Voice messaging isn't just someone saying, "You have 954 messages!" (You really need to check your voice mail more often.) Some companies offer services featuring celebrity impersonations and other character voices, and as this technology continues to grow, so will opportunities for voice professionals. Becoming employed in this field usually requires representation by an agent who shepherds artists to companies to do this kind of work.

Toys

Talking Elmo was the hottest-selling talking toy of its time when it came out. Husbands, wives, and children were literally knocking each other out trying to buy this techno-marvel. Powered by a voice chip with prerecorded voice messages that would play when you pressed a button on Elmo's tummy, Elmo spouted many verbal gems to inspire and entertain little children and grandparents, who got their jollies out of watching the wee tykes wear the batteries down.

The demand for talking toys does not appear likely to die a quick death as it did for the Pet Rock. The age of technology is transforming the toy business in ways its forefathers never thought possible.

Finding work in this field requires an agent or agency that represents voice artists and is established in the industry.

Computer and Video Games

Computer and video games feature not only great visual effects and fast-paced action, but also characters that talk and say intelligible things like "Watch out!" when a building explodes or, if you press the wrong button, "Loser!" Nobody likes losing, especially when the game you're playing rubs it in. But the truth is, many individuals are supplying voices today for computer and video game manufacturers, who can't produce these games fast enough to meet the demands of the market . . . and voice artists who need the work!

Tapping into this marketplace is tough. Usually voice artists who have an agent or are represented by a talent agency audition and land these jobs.

If none of these work out, perhaps you could become a prickly pear cactus jelly salesperson. Good ones are in short supply, and your success rate may be better, though the pay isn't all that great.

Change Is Inevitable—but Success Is Yours

Just remember that change is inevitable, except from a vending machine. Even so, success can be yours so long as you keep up with trends and work in those fields that offer the best opportunities for growth and that allow you to develop your fabulous voice personality. Opportunities continue to abound for professionals, and the list is growing every day. What you do today with your voice, you may not do a year from now or five years from now. So establishing yourself in many different fields of interest will help you sustain the kind of success you always thought was possible with your voice.

Obviously, there may be a few bumps in the road now and then. That's to be expected. But remember, confidence will breed success so

How to Make a 1/2 Million Dollars as a Mime
(Without Hardly Trying)

If all else fails, buy a copy of our next book, *How to Make a ½ Million Dollars as a Mime (Without Hardly Trying)* by Gary Owens with Jeff Lenburg, with a foreword by Marcel Marceau. Order your copy today!

BY GARY OWENS & JEFF LENBURG
~Foreword by Marcel Marceau~

This offer has expired. Not that this is a real book anyway. Of course, if you have made a ½ million dollars as a mime, then maybe you should write this book instead of us.

Photo of Gary Owens courtesy of Schlatter-Friendly-Romart.

long as you stay committed to your goal. Keeping that wonderful sense of humor of yours will get you through any rough spots. My friend and former "Laugh-In" costar Goldie Hawn said it best. She said, "Once you can laugh at your own weaknesses, you can move forward. Comedy breaks down walls. It opens up people. If you're good, you can fill up those openings with something positive."

Or as the great Will Rogers once said, "Everything is funny as long as it is happening to someone else." Remember, other people have been through experiences much like yours, the same sorts of ups and downs, and today are enjoying the success they always imagined because they

never gave up. They believed in themselves and their talent and perse-
vered no matter how big the obstacle — or how big the oncoming glacier.

Before you know it, you will make the millions you always dreamed
about and a lot more where that came from. Whether you become a
famous disc jockey, newscaster, sportscaster, dialectician, television
announcer, narrator, or weather forecaster; do voices in commercials and
animated cartoons; emcee and do public speaking; or all of the above,
keep plugging away. As a sage philosopher once said, "Luck comes to those
who are prepared."

I am certain about one thing. With your own voice, having the right
attitude and following everything suggested in this enriching abstract will
put you on the path to vocal riches. Good luck, and remember, never run
down the street with reindeer antlers in your mouth!

Voice-Over Workshops and Seminars

The following is a partial list, with Web addresses, of the leading voice-over workshops for animated cartoons, commercials, and announcing offered in the United States and Canada. For other voice-over classes, contact the telecommunications department of any college, university, institute, technical college, or trade school in your area that offers graduate programs in broadcasting, film, television, or animation.

California

Dick Orkin's Radio Ranch
radio-ranch.com
Prolific creator of humorous award-winning radio spots for local, regional, and national advertisers, Dick Orkin and creative director Christine Coyle share their talents and knowledge with several voice workshops each month, including intensive all-day, one-day, Saturday voice-over classes on the third and fourth Saturday of the month. The two-day Orkin/O'Day Annual Radio Creative Summit is held every summer in Los Angeles.

Kalmenson & Kalmenson Voice Casting
kalmenson.com

Owned and operated by Harvey and Cathy Kalmenson, Kalmenson & Kalmenson Voice Casting offers one of the most comprehensive curricula for the study of voice-over acting for nonactors, established voice actors, young voice actors (ages 8–12 and 13–17), and working professionals. Classes are conducted in its Burbank facility.

M J Productions
creatingvoices.com

Owner, voice-over director, and teacher M. J. Lallo conducts voice workshops specializing in voice-over training and voice acting. Private training also is available.

Susan Blu Workshops
Blupka Productions, Inc.
toonvoices.com/blu.html

Voice-over workshops are taught by Susan Blu, actor, director, casting director, and author of *Word of Mouth*, in all levels (beginning, intermediate, and advanced) for animation, commercials, promos and announcing, winning an audition, and more.

Voice One
vone@aol.com

Since 1986, Voice One has provided comprehensive training in voice-over, improvisation, on-camera, and stage acting. Owner/founder Elaine Clark is a working actor, casting director, published author, communications coach, and certified teacher.

Voicetrax San Francisco
voiceover-training.com

One of the nation's premier casting agencies devoted exclusively to voice-over, Voicetrax offers a comprehensive voice-over training program, comprising nearly one hundred different lectures, workshops, and seminars for both beginniners and advanced students.

Voicetrax West

voicetraxwest.com

Cindy Akers and Laurie Kaiser offer innovative classes taught by the leading professionals in the business. Producers, casting agents, directors, and working professionals provide firsthand perspective on auditioning, interpreting copy, and booking the job. Ginny McSwain, a voice actor and casting director, also holds an intensive, six-week animation voice workshop for three hours, once a week.

Voices Voicecasting

voicesvoicecasting.com

Billing itself as "L.A.'s premier voiceover casting facility," Voices Voicecasting provides voices for TV, radio, film, animation, CD-ROM, and more, plus workshops, from beginning to advanced, headed by Mary Lynn Wissner, casting director and owner.

The Voice Factory

thevoicefactory.com

One of California's premier voice-casting agencies, The Voice Factory offers a range of workshops for novices or working actors, from a low-impact two-hour introductory course to advanced programs.

The Voicecaster

voicecaster.com

Established over twenty-five years ago, The Voicecaster is the largest voice-casting company in the country, having casted over fifteen thousand projects and provided more than thirty-nine thousand performance roles for voice actors in commercial, animation, film, CD-ROM, and narration. They offer a series of voice-over workshops aimed at beginner, intermediate, and advanced students, conducted by The Voicecaster directors and the company's owner, Huck Liggett.

The Voiceover Connection, Inc.
voconnection.com
Founder and president Dolores Diehl has taught voice acting to more than one hundred thousand men, women, and children in live classes and professional audiences. Her voice-over academy offers voice workshops in animated cartoons, commercials, narration, and audiobook reading.

Wally Burr Recording
wallyburr.com
Wally Burr is a veteran director for Hanna-Barbera and producer-director with ad agency Leo Burnett (whose clients have included Kellogg's, Procter & Gamble, Pillsbury, Green Giant, Starkist, and more). He has directed hundreds of episodes of many well-known animated cartoon series, including "Conan the Barbarian," "Inspector Gadget," "G.I. Joe," "Jem," "My Little Pony," and "Transformers." Burr conducts voice-over workshops at his studio.

Illinois

Act One
actone.com
Classes in commercial, industrial film, ear prompter, TV and film, acting, voice-over, private coaching.

The Audition Studio
theauditionstudio.com
The most recommended professional training center in Chicago since 1981, The Audition Studio offers workshops that demystify the actor's process and provide a path of creative discovery for actors, based upon the twelve guideposts of Michael Shurtleff, well-known teacher, casting director, and author of the actor's "bible," *Audition*.

Chicago Actors Studio
actors-studio.net
This well-known studio offers workshops and classes for beginners to working professionals in characterizations, voice, diction, auditions, commercials, and more.

New York

Elisabeth Noone
Access Talent, Inc.
liz-noone.com
Considered one of the leading professional voice-over coaches in the industry, Liz Noone offers workshops in voice-over performance technique for beginners and advanced voice actors, and one-day narration workshops.

Voice Actors of New York
http://voiceactorsofnewyork.com
Voice Actors of New York is world renowned for offering intensive voice-over seminars and workshops. Keith Mannino and Jamie Lee head cutting-edge courses that also include New York City casting directors and agents.

Voiceovers Unlimited
voiceoversunlimited.com
With over twenty years in the business, Voiceovers Unlimited offers cartoon and film dubbing/looping workshops with Pamela Lewis, New York City's top coach in this field; audition and monologue workshops with theater, film, and TV casting directors and agents; voice and diction workshops; and private coaching sessions.

Canada

Voiceworx
voiceworx.com
Founded by twelve-time Clio Award winner and commercial voice actor
Mike Kirby, this training and production facility is for performers wishing
to pursue a career in commercial voice-over work. Voiceworx provides in-
studio workshops, conducted by professional performers, directors, and
producers who make their living in the performing arts, in radio and television commercial voice-over, documentary and corporate video narration, cartoon voice, character multivoice, and studio protocol, in a
state-of-the-art recording studio.

Talent Agencies

The following is a partial listing of various SAG- and AFTRA-authorized talent agencies throughout the United States and around the world that represent voice-over talent:

Alaska

Alaska Models and Talent
601 W. Forty-first Ave.
Anchorage, AK 99503-6652
Phone: 907-561-5739

Cup'ik Warrior Productions
PO Box 110662
Anchorage, AK 99511-0662
Phone: 907-258-2454
cupik@cupikwarrior.com
cupikwarrior.com

Northern Stars Casting & Theatre Services
PO Box 770369
Eagle River, AK 99577
Phone: 907-688-1370

Scout/Alaska: Talent Scout
3939 Turnagain Blvd., East
Anchorage, AK 99517
Phone: 907-248-7500

Stanley Talent & Production Co.
55630 Silverado Way
Anchorage, AK 99518-1653
Phone: 907-561-6877

Arizona

Dani's Agency
One E. Camelback Rd., #550
Phoenix, AZ 85012
Phone: 602-263-1918
danisagency.com

Ford/Robert Black Agency
4300 N. Miller Rd., Suite 202
Scottsdale, AZ 85251
Phone: 480-966-2537
fordrobertblackagency.com

Fosi's Modeling & Talent Agency
2777 N. Campbell Ave., #209
Tucson, AZ 85719
Phone: 520-795-3534

Signature Models & Talent Agency
2600 N. Forty-fourth St., #209
Phoenix, AZ 85008
Phone: 480-966-1102
signaturemodelsandtalent.com

Arkansas

The Agency, Inc.
802 W. Eighth St.
Little Rock, AR 72201
Phone: 501-374-8903

California

Abrams Artists Agency
9200 Sunset Blvd., #407
Los Angeles, CA 90069
Phone: 310-859-1417

Acme/PoSH Voices
4727 Wilshire Blvd., Suite 333
Los Angeles, CA 90010
Phone: 323-602-0370
voicebank.net

Alvarado Rey
8455 Beverly Blvd., #410
Los Angeles, CA 90048
Phone: 323-655-7978

Arlene Thornton & Associates
12711 Ventura Blvd., Suite 490
Studio City, CA 91604
Phone: 818-760-6688

BTG
6500 Wilshire Blvd., Suite 2210
Los Angeles, CA 90048
Phone: 323-852-9559

Cassell-Levy, Inc.
843 N. Sycamore Ave.
Los Angeles, CA 90038
Phone: 323-461-3971

Coast to Coast Talent Group
3350 Barham Blvd.
Los Angeles, CA 90068
Phone: 323-845-9200

Cunningham-Escott-Dipene (CED) Talent Agency
10635 Santa Monica Blvd., #130
Los Angeles, CA 90025
Phone: 310-475-2111
cedvoices.com

Daniel Hoff Agency
1800 N. Highland Ave., Suite 300
Hollywood, CA 90028
Phone: 323-962-6643

Gold Liedtke & Associates
3500 W. Olive Ave., Suite 1400
Burbank, CA 91505
Phone: 818-972-4334

Hervey/Grimes Talent Agency
10561 Missouri Ave., #2
Los Angeles, CA 90025
Phone: 310-475-2010

Hollander Talent Group
14011 Ventura Blvd., #202
Sherman Oaks, CA 91423
Phone: 818-382-9800

Imperium 7
9911 W. Pico Blvd., Suite 1290
Los Angeles, CA 90035
Phone: 310-203-9009

Independent Artists Agency, Inc.
9200 Sunset Blvd., Suite 805
Los Angeles, CA 90069
Phone: 310-550-5000

Innovative Artists
1505 Tenth St.
Santa Monica, CA 90401
Phone: 310-553-5200

International Creative Management
8942 Wilshire Blvd., #155
Beverly Hills, CA 90211
Phone: 310-550-4304

JE Talent, LLC
323 Geary St., #302
San Francisco, CA 94102
Phone: 415-395-9475

JLA Talent
9151 Sunset Blvd.
West Hollywood, CA 90069
Phone: 310-276-5677

Kazarian/Spencer & Associates
11365 Ventura Blvd., #100
Studio City, CA 91604
Phone: 818-769-9111

Look Talent
166 Geary St.
San Francisco, CA 94108
Phone: 415-781-2841

Sandie Schnarr Talent
8500 Melrose Ave., #212
West Hollywood, CA 90069
Phone: 310-360-7680

The Savage Agency
6212 Banner Ave.
Los Angeles, CA 90038
Phone: 323-461-8316

Special Artists Agency
345 N. Maple Dr.
Beverly Hills, CA 90210
Phone: 310-859-9688

Stars Agency
23 Grant, 4th Floor
San Francisco, CA 94108
Phone: 415-421-6272

Sutton, Barth & Vennari
145 S. Fairfax Ave., #310
Los Angeles, CA 90036
Phone: 323-938-6000
sbvtalentagency.com

Tisherman Agency
6767 Forest Lawn Dr., #101
Los Angeles, CA 90068
Phone: 323-850-6767

Voicebank Test Talent Agency Account
543 N. La Cienega Blvd., Suite 201
Los Angeles, CA 90048
Phone: 310-854-6712
voicebank.net

VOX, Inc.
5670 Wilshire Blvd., Suite #820
Los Angeles, CA 90036
Phone: 323-852-9559

William Morris Agency
151 El Camino Dr.
Beverly Hills, CA 90212
Phone: 310-859-4085
wma.com

Colorado

Aspire Model & Talent, Inc.
516 Acoma St.
Denver, CO 80204
Phone: 303-733-3888
aspireagency.com

Big Fish Talent Representation
312 W. First Ave.
Denver, CO 80223-1510
Phone: 303-744-7170
bigfishtalent.com

Connecticut

Maresca Talent Agency
PO Box 2212
Branford, CT 06405
Phone: 203-481-0547

Florida

Alexa Model & Talent Management, Inc.
4100 W. Kennedy Blvd., #228
Tampa, FL 33609
Phone: 813-286-8281

Anderson Greene Entertainment, Inc.
1210 Washington Ave., #245
Miami Beach, FL 33139
Phone: 305-674-9881

Arthur Arthur, Inc.
6542 U.S. Highway 41 North, Suite 205 A
Apollo Beach, FL 33572
Phone: 813-645-9700
Fax: 813-645-9797

Azuree Talent, Inc.
140 N. Orlando Ave., Suite 120
Winter Park, FL 32789
Phone: 407-629-5025

Berg Agency, Inc.
PO Box 274187
Tampa, FL 33688
Phone: 813-877-5533

Boca Talent & Model Management
829 SE Ninth Street
Deerfield Beach, FL 33441
Phone: 954-428-4677
bca1000@aol.com

Brevard Talent Group, Inc.
405 Palm Springs Blvd.
Indian Harbor Beach, FL 32937
Phone: 321-773-1355

The Sandi Bell Talent Agency
2582 S. Maguire Rd., #171
Ocoee, FL 34761
Phone: 407-445-9221
Fax: 407-445-0549

Strictly Speaking
711 Executive Dr.
Winter Park, FL 32789
Phone: 407-645-2111
strictlyspeakinginc.com

Georgia

Premier Casting
PO Box 76961
Atlanta, GA 30358
Phone: 770-202-7619
Fax: 770-938-6440
premiercasting@yahoo.com

The Voice Casting Network
8950 Laurel Way
Alpharetta, GA 30022-5938
Phone: 1-877-449-1689
voicecasting.com

Hawaii

ADR Model & Talent Agency
419 Waiakamilo Rd., Suite 204–205
Honolulu, HI 96817
Phone: 808-842-1313

Kathy Muller Talent Agency
619 Kapahulu Ave., Penthouse
Honolulu, HI 96815
Phone: 808-737-7917

V. Talent & Model Management, Inc.
2153 N. King St., #323-A
Honolulu, HI 96819
Phone: 808-842-0881
vtalent@hawaii.rr.com

Idaho

Blanche B. Evans Agency International
4311 Audubon Pl.
Boise, ID 83705-3851
Phone: 208-344-5380

Idaho Modeling & Talent Agency
2090 S. Cole Rd., Suite D
Boise, ID 83709
Phone: 208-672-9515

Metcalf Modeling & Talent Agency
1851 S. Century Way, Suite 3
Boise, ID 83709
Phone: 208-378-8777
Fax: 208-327-0651
metcalfagt@qwest.net

Michelle's Talent Agency
808 Green Dr.
Pocatello, ID 83204
Phone: 208-234-4035
michellestalent@aol.com

Palmer Talent
PO Box 750
Ketchum, ID 83340
Phone: 208-788-4501
Fax: 208-788-6159
palmer@sunvalley.net

Talent Pool
PO Box 8322
Boise, ID 83707
Phone: 208-384-1707

Illinois

Encore Talent Agency
700 N. Sacramento Blvd., Suite 221
Chicago, IL 60612
Phone: 773-638-7300

Geddes Agency
1633 N. Halsted
Chicago, IL 60614
Phone: 312-787-8333

Lily's Talent Agency
1301 W. Washington, Suite B
Chicago, IL 60607
Phone: 312-601-2345
lilystalent.com

Linda Jack Talent
230 E. Ohio, #200
Chicago, IL 60611
Phone: 312-587-1155

Naked Voices
865 N. Sangamon, Suite 415
Chicago, IL 60622
Phone: 312-563-0136
nakedvoices.com

Shirley Hamilton, Inc.
333 E. Ontario, Suite 302
Chicago, IL 60611
Phone: 312-787-4700
shirleyhamilton.com

Stewart Talent Agency
58 W. Huron
Chicago, IL 60610
Phone: 312-943-3131
stewarttalent.com

Voices Unlimited
541 N. Fairbanks Ct., #2735
Chicago, IL 60611
Phone: 312-832-1113
voicesunlimited.com

Michigan

The Group Model & Talent Mgmt.
29540 Southfield Rd., Suite 200
Southfield, MI 48076
Phone: 248-552-8842
theigroup.com

Nykole Lynn Talent, LLC
29200 Southfield Rd., Suite 202
Southfield, MI 48076
Phone: 248-552-3700
Fax: 248-552-9603
info@nykolelynn.com

Minnesota

Lipservice, Inc.
2010 E. Hennepin Ave., Suite 8-125
Minneapolis, MN 55413
Phone: 612-338-5477

Moore Creative Talent
1610 W. Lake St.
Minneapolis, MN 55408
Phone: 612-455-6714
mooretalent.com

Wehmann Models/Talent, Inc.
1128 Harmon Pl., #205
Minneapolis, MN 55403
Phone: 612-333-6393
www.wehmann.com

Missouri

I & I Agency, LLC
1509 Westport Rd., Suite 200
Kansas City, MO 64111
Phone: 816-410-9950
Fax: 816-410-6944

Montana

Adams/O'Connell Talent Agency
801 E. Sixth Ave.
Helena, MT 59601
Phone: 406-443-7547

Creative World Model and Talent Agency
PO Box 50177
Billings, MT 59105
Phone: 406-259-9540

Entertainment Connection, Inc.
PO Box 50596
Billings, MT 59105
Phone: 406-259-6600

Maxie's Agency
PO Box 289
Clancy, MT 59634
Phone: 406-761-1559

MMTA: Montana's Model & Talent Agency
1332 Wine Glass La.
Livingston, MT 59047
Phone: 406-222-4699
Fax: 406-222-9390

N.A.S.S. Talent Management/All Faces Model & Talent Agency
PO Box 3900
Bozeman, MT 59772
Phone: 406-586-7045
Fax: 406-586-4774
nastalentmanagement.com

New Jersey

Models on the Move Model & Talent Agency
1200 Rt. 70
Barclay Towers, Suite 6
PO Box 4037
Cherry Hill, NJ 08034
Phone: 856-667-1060

Veronica Goodman Agency
PO Box 1535
Cherry Hill, NJ 08002
Phone: 856-795-3133

New York

Abrams Artists Agency
275 Seventh Ave., 26th Floor
New York, NY 10001
Phone: 646-486-4600

Access Talent
37 E. Twenty-eighth St., Suite 500
New York, NY 10016-7919
Phone: 212-331-9600
accesstalent.com

Ann Wright Representatives
165 W. Forty-sixth St., #1105
New York, NY 10036
Phone: 212-764-6770

Arcieri & Associates
305 Madison Ave., #2315
New York, NY 10165
Phone: 212-286-1700

Atlas Talent
36 W. Forty-fourth St., Suite 1000
New York, NY 10036
Phone: 212-730-4500
atlastalent.com

Cunningham-Escott-Dipene (CED) Talent Agency
257 Park Ave., South, 9th Floor
New York, NY 10010
Phone: 212-477-1666
cedvoices.com

Don Buchwald & Associates, Inc.
10 East Forty-fourth St.
New York, NY 10017
Phone: 212-867-1070
buchwald.com

Ingber & Associates
274 Madison Ave., Suite 1104
New York, NY 10016
Phone: 212-889-9450

Innovative Artists
235 Park Ave., South, 7th Floor
New York, NY 10003
Phone: 212-253-6900

International Creative Management
40 W. Fifty-seventh St.
New York, NY 10019
Phone: 212-556-5629

Paradigm
500 Fifth Ave., 37th Floor
New York, NY 10110
Phone: 212-703-7540

Tamar Wolbrom, Inc.
130 W. Forty-second St., Suite 707
New York, NY 10036
Phone: 212-398-4595
tamarw.com

William Morris Agency
1325 Avenue of the Americas
New York, NY 10019
Phone: 212-903-1195
wma.com

North Carolina

Stars Talent Network, Inc.
PO Box 99588
Raleigh, NC 27624-9588
Phone: 919-529-1170
Fax: 919-529-1171

Oregon

Erhart Talent
037 SW Hamilton St.
Portland, OR 97201
Phone: 503-243-6362

Ryan Artists
239 NW Thirteenth Ave., Suite 213
Portland, OR 97209
Phone: 503-274-1005
Fax: 503-274-0907
ryanartists.com

Ursa Talent, LLC
1310 Coburg Rd., Suite 10
Eugene, OR 97401
Phone: 541-485-4495
Fax: 541-726-6591
contact@ursatalent.com
ursatalent.com

Pennsylvania

Greer Lange Association, Inc.
40 Lloyd Ave., Suite 104
Malvern, PA 19355
Phone: 610-647-5515

GWA (G. Williams Agency)
525 S. Fourth St., #365
Philadelphia, PA 19147
Phone: 215-627-9533

Mary Anne Claro Talent Agency, Inc.
1513 W. Passyunk Ave.
Philadelphia, PA 19145
Phone: 215-465-7788

Plaza 7
160 N. Gulph Rd.
King of Prussia, PA 19406
Phone: 616-337-2693
Fax: 616-337-4762

Reinhard Talent Agency, Inc.
2021 Arch St., Suite 400
Philadelphia, PA 19103
Phone: 215-567-2000

South Carolina

Agency South Entertainment
1605 Pincushion Rd.
Columbia, SC 29209
Phone: 803-647-7789
agencysouth@aol.com

Tennessee

Actors and Others Talent
6676 Memphis-Arlington Rd.
Bartlett, TN 38135
Phone: 901-377-5527

Agency for the Performing Arts
3017 Poston Ave.
Nashville, TN 37203
Phone: 615-297-0100
Fax: 615-297-5434

Texas

DB Talent
7402 Brodie La.
Austin, TX 78745
Phone: 512-292-1030
dbtalent.com

Kim Dawson Agency
2710 N. Stemmons Way, #700
Dallas, TX 75207-2208
Phone: 214-630-5161

Mary Collins Agency
2909 Cole Ave., #250
Dallas, TX 75204
Phone: 214-871-8900
marycollins.com

Pastorini-Bosby Talent
3013 Fountainview, #240
Houston, TX 77057
Phone: 713-266-4488
pbtalent.com

Utah

Revolution Talent
4500 S. 565 E, Suite A 100
Salt Lake City, UT 84107
Phone: 801-747-3261
Fax: 801-747-3122

Talent Management Group, Inc.
339 E. 3900 S, #202D
Salt Lake City, UT 84107
Phone: 801-263-6940
talentmg.com

Washington

Actors Group
3400 Beacon Ave. S
Seattle, WA 98144
Phone: 206-624-9465
Fax: 206-624-9466
theactorsgroup.com

Colleen Bell Modeling & Talent Agency
14205 SE Thirty-sixth St., #100
Bellevue, WA 98006
Phone: 425-649-1111
Fax: 425-649-1113
bellagency@aol.com
colleenbellagency.com

Dramatic Artists Agency
50 Sixteenth Ave.
Kirkland, WA 98033
Phone: 425-827-4147
Fax: 425-827-1948
dramaticartists.com

Topo Swope Talent
1932 First Ave., Suite 700
Seattle, WA 98101
Phone: 206-443-2021
Fax: 206-443-7648
topo@toposwopetalent.com
toposwopetalent.com

Wisconsin

Arlene Wilson Management
807 N. Jefferson St.
Milwaukee, WI 53202
Phone: 414-283-5600
arlenewilson.com

Lori Lins, Ltd.
7611 W. Holmes Ave.
Milwaukee, WI 53220
Phone: 414-282-3500
lorilins.com

Canada

Characters Talent Agency
8 Elm St.
Toronto, Ontario M5G 1G7
Canada
Phone: 416-964-8522

Edna Talent Management, Ltd.
318 Dundas St., West
Toronto, Ontario M5T 1G5
Canada
Phone: 416-413-7800
etmltd.com

Fountainhead Talent, Inc.
2 Pardee Ave., Suite 204
Toronto, Ontario M6K 3H5
Canada
Phone: 416-538-6888
fountainheadtalent.com

Fusion Artists, Inc.
401 Richmond St., West, Suite 401
Toronto, Ontario M5V 3A8
Canada
Phone: 416-408-3304

Jordan & Associates
615 Yonge St., Suite 401
Toronto, Ontario M4Y 1Z5
Canada
Phone: 416-515-2028

Lucas Talent, Inc.
100 W. Pender St., 7th Floor
Vancouver, British Columbia V6B 1R8
Canada
Phone: 604-685-0345
lucastalent.com

Noble Caplan Agency
1260 Yonge St., 2nd Floor
Toronto, Ontario M4T 1W6
Canada
Phone: 416-920-5385

Oscars Abrams Zimel & Associates
438 Queen St., East
Toronto, Ontario M5A 1T4
Canada
Phone: 416-860-1790

Pacific Artists Management
1404-510 W. Hastings St.
Vancouver, British Columbia V6B 1L8
Canada
Phone: 604-688-4077

England

Hobsons Talent Agency
62 Chiswick High Rd.
Chiswick, London W4 1SY
England
Phone: 011-44-0-208-9953628

Ireland

All Mouth
27 Upper Mount St.
Dublin, Dublin 2
Ireland
Phone: 011-353-1-6383295

Index

About the Authors

Gary Owens is one of the most recognizable names and voices in show business today. Inducted into not one, but three distinguished halls of fame for radio and television, he has a rich, compelling baritone voice that has entertained radio and television audiences for many years in animated cartoons, commercials, and motion pictures and on television shows and specials.

Ever since being pushed into the national spotlight as the on-camera announcer on TV's "Rowan and Martin's Laugh-In," Gary has enjoyed phenomenal success with his voice. Honored as the Top Radio Personality in the United States and Top Radio Personality in the World by *Billboard* and *Radio & Records* magazines, he has hosted twelve thousand local and national radio shows. He has also starred in more than one thousand network television shows and specials (and been a regular on sixteen series), voiced over three thousand animated cartoons, including "Roger Ramjet," "Space Ghost and Dino Boy," "The Ren and Stimpy Show," and "Buzz Lightyear," and appeared in seventeen motion pictures.

In addition, Gary has been a top promo announcer for every major television network. He has been featured in over thirty thousand commercials for radio and television, lent his voice to numerous videos and DVDs (Richard Jones's Emmy Award–winning "Dinosaurs" series, which Gary hosts with Eric Boardman, has sold more than five hundred thousand copies on videotape), narrated dozens of audiobooks (about Bill Cosby and many others), appeared on fifteen record albums and CDs, and been nominated for six Grammy Awards. Furthermore, Gary has served as the master of ceremonies and hosted thousands of Hollywood events, including major movie premieres and charity shows.

Gary has been recognized with a star on the Hollywood Walk of Fame (next to Walt Disney). Also, his ear print is encased in cement at NBC Studios in "beautiful downtown Burbank," a signature phrase coined by Gary. Gary's first book sold more than seven hundred thousand copies for Price Stern and Sloan. It was the start of the elephant jokes: *Elephants, Grapes, and Pickles*. His second book, *The Gary Owens What to Do While Holding the Phonebook*, was a hit trivia hardback!

Jeff Lenburg is an award-winning celebrity biographer and entertainment historian. He is the author of fourteen nonfiction books that have been translated into several foreign languages and have also been nominated for several awards as well, including the American Library Association's Best Non-Fiction Award and the Evangelical Christian Publisher Association's Gold Medallion Award for Best Autobiography/Biography.

His books include *All the Gold in California and Other Places, People and Things*, the autobiography of singer-songwriter Larry Gatlin; *The Encyclopedia of Animated Cartoons*; *Once a Stooge, Always a Stooge*, the autobiography of Three Stooges member Joe Besser; *Peekaboo: The Story of Veronica Lake*; *The Three Stooges Scrapbook*; *The Great Cartoon Directors*; and many others.

During his career, Jeff has interviewed dozens of other major personalities, world figures, sports legends, and headline makers, including tennis champ Chris Evert, former first lady Betty Ford, and baseball great Nolan Ryan.

Jeff has appeared on hundreds of radio and television programs, including "BBC Live," NBC's "Today Show," "Entertainment Tonight," CNN's "Showbiz Today," and E!'s "Mysteries & Scandals."